TOMMY at 50

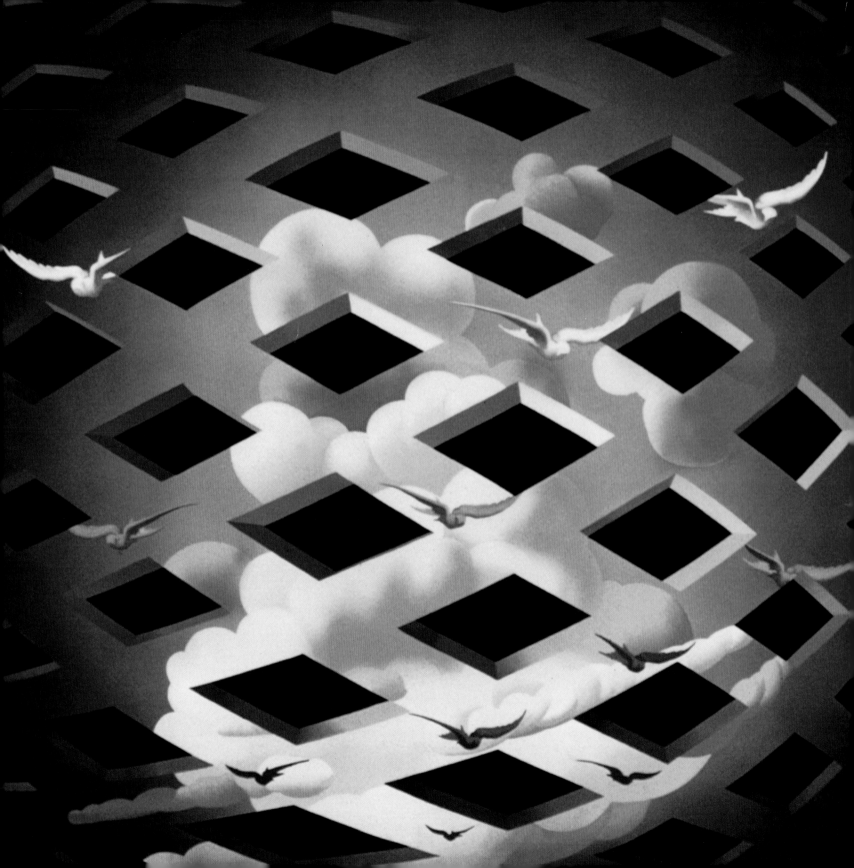

TOMMY at 50

The Mood, the Music, the Look, and the Legacy
of The Who's Legendary Rock Opera

Chris Charlesworth and Mike McInnerney
Foreword by Pete Townshend

APOLLO
PUBLISHERS

contents

1 the mood   12

A deep dive into the world that the members of The Who found themselves in during 1968–1969, and the themes and ideas that fed into the creation of their defining work.

2 the music   48

Inside the creation of the songs that make up *Tommy*, from the earliest sketches in Pete Townshend's home studio to the fully realized versions heard on the record.

3 the look   86

An immersive exploration of *Tommy*'s beautifully designed, triple-gatefold record cover, how it was created, and the ideas that informed and inspired it.

4 the legacy   122

Tommy then and now: a chronicle of the ways these songs and ideas have been remade and remodeled over the years, onstage, onscreen, and beyond.

foreword

by Pete Townshend

Mike McInnerney was an important figure in my life in the late sixties. His move to Richmond, and later to East Twickenham near the River Thames, attracted me to the area. When we got married my wife Karen and I bought a house near Mike and his wife, Katie. They were a gregarious couple. Their hippie wedding in Hyde Park made the national papers, and their dilapidated but aristocratic flat was always full of life.

Mike worked constantly under a single ordinary light bulb. He entertained and pontificated from his drawing board at one side of the room, stopping only to eat. I felt envious that he could work and socialize at once. I needed earphones and solitude for my recording. Behind him on the wall was a picture of the young, craggy-looking spiritual sage Meher Baba. I was curious, and Mike gave me a book called *The God-Man*. I was stimulated and shaken by the book, and over the next few years made an academic study of the Indian Master. I never really stopped to think; I was swept along, I felt I was simply catching up with knowledge I already had, but had forgotten.

It was in this mood that we began work on *Tommy*. I conceived the basis for the story quite suddenly when I heard myself say one day that a normal man was effectively deaf, dumb, and blind when faced with spiritual truth. I couldn't quite see how Mike was going to produce a visualization of the idea, but we sat to talk about it. Characteristically, Mike's response was enthusiastically positive. He overflowed with visual ideas, many of them influencing the way some of the songs—at that time in raw demo form—were to evolve and finally land.

A few months later, I presented Mike with the first rough demo assembly on cassette tape. He set to work, and the rest became a tangible testimony to Mike's genius and speed. As an illustrator, he was constantly up against impossible deadlines, and in the case of *Tommy* he worked indefatigably to produce the cover art, even though the actual album completion was continually delayed by technical and financial problems.

I felt we had been at one in our vision of the disaffected and tragically de-spiritualized postwar child. In the punk rock era it became an amusement to ridicule the children of the sixties as silly hippies, complaining ones at that. But there was real pain beneath the pleasure-seeking. In *Tommy* I tried to reveal the sense of futility carried by many postwar children. Despite the fact that we had never-had-it-so-good, growing up at a time when the global map was still half-pink, we felt destitute. We loved our parents. We admired their courage during the war. We grieved for all those lost. But there was something missing. Terrible mistakes had been made.

I think the international achievements of so many young people from this era bely the idea that we were spoilt brats who simply used precious peace-time for pleasure. We knew we were lucky and that our opportunities were unique. I think this made us feel a responsibility to do more than make money, have families, and be happy. We wanted to effect a shift in the spiritual attitudes of everyone in the West. For my part I knew that something very special had started to happen when we performed as The Who; it seemed more than the effect of marijuana that created the congregational atmosphere that we were often able to spark.

It is touching to be reminded of all this. What Mike writes here feels to me to be brand new, entirely surprising—London as a city being shaken up by hippie revolutionaries with no money and their brains partly fried. We were really taking on New York and San Francisco I think. To be honest, it's clear I missed most of it driving up and down the M1 in the rain and snow.

Mike's contribution to this book is a really vitally needed contribution to the background of how *Tommy* came to be. I joked with Mike that

the rest of it—assembled by Chris Charlesworth, a trusted friend, author, editor, and publisher—based to a great extent on articles, reviews, interviews, and biographies previously published, will itself be researched and pillaged by other writers over and over again for the next two hundred years or more. That seems disparaging. But I always wanted my work to be taken seriously, so I really can't complain. I have to be held to account not only for what

I do creatively, but for what I set out to do, what I actually achieved, what I said about it later, and the way that I responded to criticism, especially charges of being pretentious.

I'm delighted this collection adds new input. With *Tommy*, as with various Who projects that followed, I took massive risks. I was not alone of course. By some miracle *Tommy* came off, and Mike's beautiful artwork for the foldout album sleeve was a huge part of its success.

introduction

by Chris Charlesworth

As *Sgt. Pepper* is to The Beatles, *Tommy* is to The Who. It is the album that elevated them to rock's high table, the album that rescued them from penury, and the album for which, whether they like it or not, they are still best known and revered.

Tommy **radiates elegance and flair.** It's a rich, expansive, and thoughtful mix of Pete Townshend's compositional ideas and spiritual ideals, certainly mellower in timbre than anything his group had recorded up to that point, yet at the same time far more profound, more rewarding, and, as the passage of time has demonstrated, more enduring.

To find out where it came from and how it came about, we need first of all to examine where the four members of The Who came from and where they found themselves in 1969, the year that *Tommy* was released, and this calls for a brief resume of their career up to that point.

Remarkably for a quartet that would be acclaimed as one of the world's greatest ever rock bands, three members—guitarist and songwriter Peter Townshend, singer Roger Daltrey, and bass player John Entwistle—all attended the same secondary school as teenagers in the West London suburb of Acton, close to where they were raised. In 1960, Daltrey, a bequiffed, rough-around-the-edges rocker at heart, formed a skiffle group that he fronted on a cheap f-hole guitar. Around about the same time, Townshend, a mixed-up thinker seeking the meaning of life, and Entwistle, a gifted musical prodigy, were playing banjo and French horn, respectively, in a rival trad-jazz outfit. Both came from families with musical backgrounds. By 1961, they were playing in schoolboy bands, with Townshend on guitar and Entwistle using a bass guitar he had built himself.

One day in 1961, Daltrey spotted Entwistle toting his bass guitar in the street and invited him to join his group, enticing him with the guarantee of imbursement. Not long afterward, Entwistle recommended Townshend join, too. Daltrey acquiesced. The nucleus of The Who now in place, they performed locally for two years as The Detours, playing covers of popular hits in pubs and social clubs before graduating to R&B. Daltrey worked in a sheet-metal factory, Entwistle in a tax office, and Townshend became an art student, but by the end of 1963 the group had become their main focus. Keith Moon, an animated ball of confusion, joined them on drums in April of 1964, adding a defining spring to their step. Later that year, they were taken on by managers Kit Lambert and Chris Stamp, a couple of seat-of-the-pants opportunists from the film industry whose enthusiasm and ingenuity somehow kept the show on the road, despite everyone's chronic inability to live within their means—not least Townshend and Moon, who had taken to climaxing stage shows by wrecking their equipment in the name of art.

From the outset, The Who—as they were properly known from the autumn of 1964 onward—concentrated on performing live. In those days, this was the only way to make a living. A tally of exactly how many shows The Detours/Who played in their earliest days is difficult to confirm, but it is likely that the group played at least one hundred shows before Moon's arrival, and more than sixty during the remainder of 1964. Thereafter, there were around 230 in 1965, 200 in 1966, 180-plus in 1967, 120 in 1968, and twenty-five or so in early 1969, up to *Tommy*'s release in May. That's over nine hundred, an unusually large amount by anyone's standards—probably more shows than any other group of their generation, bar The Beatles before them[1]—and ample to bond them tightly together in ways that others on the live circuit simply sat back and envied.

There was something else that was unusual about The Who. Although all bar Moon could sing well, with the notable exception of Entwistle they were not the most technically proficient, nor were they the most well rehearsed or exacting of rock musicians. Precision tuning was not their style, yet, oddly enough, performing came naturally to them when they were in full flow. Like a handful of other rock acts that would come to operate at the very highest level, it was as if a hidden fifth member materialized amid the other four onstage, leading them and their audiences to a kind of rock 'n' roll paradise that others in this line of work could only dream about.

Townshend's vigorous style was certainly eye-catching, but it restricted his accuracy, and he loved to improvise, which sometimes threw the others off their stride; Moon played the drums as if they were a lead instrument, throwing himself into the music with abandon, timekeeping often forgotten; Daltrey, initially at least, had a limited range, fought hard to assert his role, and often had difficulty hearing himself above the volume. They looked to Townshend for cues, and to Entwistle for a rhythmic foundation. All bar Entwistle seemed to be playing to the crowd, Townshend with his leaps and arm-spinning windmills, Daltrey with his microphone twirling, and Moon with his facial twitches, flurries around the kit, and offbeat showmanship. Out of it all eventually came a sound and a spectacle that thrilled beyond reason, vastly more intense than other groups on the same level who sang only about sex and partying, or whose music was rooted in the blues.

The road to *Tommy*, however, was riddled with potholes. Disparate characters all, they had, among many other setbacks, weathered a bitter leadership contest between Daltrey and Townshend, a ruinous recording deal that saw their earnings diminish to petty cash, and the indignity of having to open shows for Herman's Hermits on their first American tour. What they had going for them, however, was a headstrong, reckless determination to succeed against the odds, and a wealth of experience performing together that had, in turn, fostered an unusually close awareness of each other's musical skills, strengths, and limitations.

Crucially, Lambert had from the outset encouraged Townshend to write his own songs. To this end, in 1965 he bought Townshend two stereo Vortexion tape machines on which he could record demos at home, double-tracking guitar, bass, keyboards, and drums, as well as singing. Copies of these home demos of his songs—most of them refined recordings in themselves—were then circulated to the other three members of The Who so they could learn their parts before all four assembled in the studio, usually IBC in London's Portland Place, to record the finished song. This unique method of working ensured that so long as Daltrey, Entwistle, and Moon had done their homework when they arrived at the studio to begin work, they were all well prepared.

Nevertheless, The Who's recording career was inconsistent, the group never as prolific as their peers. Their first album, released toward the end of 1965, was too jarring, too raucous, for an era dominated by smoother songs by smoother groups. Their second a year later was a patchy affair handicapped by a few inferior songs not written by Townshend or Entwistle. Their third, a dazzlingly imaginative piece of work that anticipated the

distasteful commercial sponsorship of modern-day rock, failed on release only because The Who's profile was nowhere near as high as it ought to have been. This was largely because, in the meantime, their singles had virtually dried up. Having launched themselves with an explosive burst on the pop charts—only The Kinks, with "You Really Got Me," "All Day and All of the Night," and "Tired of Waiting for You," could match "I Can't Explain," "Anyway Anyhow Anywhere," and "My Generation"—thereafter they seemed to waver, the sheer strangeness of their output baffling record

buyers. Their finest single ever, "I Can See for Miles," a visionary track released in 1967 and included on that third album, stalled at #10 in the UK charts, prompting a disillusioned Townshend to spit in disgust, "To me that was the ultimate Who record yet it didn't sell. I spat on the British record buyer."

Two further singles released by the group in 1968 failed even to crack the Top 20. The Who were at a crossroads. *Tommy*, therefore, would be their lifesaver—the record that saved them from imploding amid a welter of debts, recriminations, and resentment.

1 the mood

Mike McInnerney

the mood

The Who as a cultural force in the sixties personify the rise of youth culture. The group represented a new constituency and new voice in postwar British society—a postwar way of life in which adolescents found ways to tell their own stories. Stories that would evolve and reflect a growing confidence for self-realization and self-fulfillment—a politics of identity that would create a culture of political protest, radical experiments in alternative lifestyles, and revolutions in sexual understanding, individual rights, and spiritual enquiry.

The "Swinging London" of the mid-sixties marked an escape from the austerity and monochrome environment of Britain's postwar years and the advent of a bright, colorful, and youth-driven culture. New housing schemes were replacing many of the grimy, Victorian terraced back-to backs, transforming towns and cities across the nation; seven new "plateglass" universities (named for their distinctively modern architecture) had recently been founded; young people's access to pop and rock music had been transformed by pirate radio stations such as Radio London and Radio Caroline. (The BBC eventually caught up in 1967, when Radio 1, devoted exclusively to playing rock and pop music, went on air.)

Colorful new fashions made everything seem brighter; and theaters, movies, novels, and poetry were dealing with new subjects, from Granada TV's soap opera *Coronation Street*, first broadcast in 1960 and depicting the trials and tribulations of a working-class community in Salford, to the BBC's groundbreaking, gritty *Cathy Come Home* (1966), which dealt with homelessness and poverty. *Ready Steady Go!*, broadcast from 1963 to 1966, marked the beginning of a revolution in British rock-and-pop TV, and working-class accents could be heard regularly on BBC TV and radio and in theaters for the first time.

That the class-conscious, stiff-upper-lip hidebound Britain of old seemed to be disappearing for good was symbolized for many by the election of Prime Minister Harold Wilson's Labour Party in 1964, replacing the Conservative Party, led by the privately educated Harold Macmillan, whose government had been rocked by scandal toward the end of its life.

There was full employment, and Britain—like the United States, most of Europe, and other nations—was enjoying an economic boom. A new, positive feeling of adventure was in the air, and along with greater prosperity came an interest in exploring alternative ways of living, and thinking.

The hippie revolution, spreading from California across the Western world, brought an interest in communal living and in spiritual exploration. The Esalen Institute, the birthplace of the Human Potential movement, was founded in California in 1962 by Michael Murphy and Dick Price; Alan Watts, a leading exponent of Zen Buddhism thinking, published *The Way of Zen* in 1957; and traveling the "hippie trail" became a rite of passage, with many such adventurers seeking to learn more about Eastern religions (and, often, to smoke dope at the same time) . . .

International Times

One of the first visible signs of an emerging counterculture in London came on June 11, 1965, at the Royal Albert Hall, during a daylong poetry event, the International Poetry Incarnation, organized by writer Barry Miles and his gallerist wife Sue, photographer and activist John "Hoppy" Hopkins, filmmaker Barbara Rubin, and poets Alex Trocchi and Michael Horowitz.

The gathering of seven thousand flower-waving people listened to performances by beat poet Allen Ginsberg, author of the seminal poem "Howl"; fellow beat poet Gregory Corso; progressive poet and key counterculture figure Michael Horowitz; Simon Vinkenoog, a member of the Dutch Provos movement of cultural provocateurs;

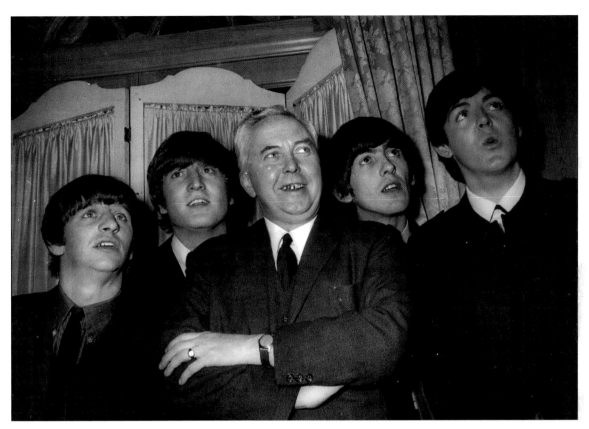

previous spread: The Who on the set of *Ready Steady Go!*, the pop TV show that launched them, August 6, 1965. Shortly after its release in May 1965, The Who's second single, "Anyway Anyhow Anywhere," was adopted by *RSG!* as its theme tune for several weeks.

top right: The Beatles with Labour Party leader and future British prime minister Harold Wilson at the Variety Club of Great Britain Awards, Dorchester Hotel, London, March 19, 1964.

bottom right: Allen Ginsberg (*center*) with fellow poets and writers Harry Fainlight, Adrian Mitchell, Alexander Trocchi, and Anselm Hollo at the Albert Memorial in South Kensington, London, June 11, 1965, prior to that evening's International Poetry Incarnation at the nearby Royal Albert Hall.

left: An outdoor food kitchen provided by The Diggers, a radical community-action group, to support the flood of young hippies arriving in the Haight-Ashbury district of San Francisco, 1966.

The Vietnam situation needs something big to happen to stop the war, either from the people of Vietnam or America. There will always be teenagers ready to throw themselves under tanks. I wonder what I would do if we were in the same position?"

Pete Townshend to *Melody Maker*, March 1966

Lawrence Ferlinghetti, co-founder of City Lights Bookshop in San Francisco; Adrian Mitchell, with his powerful reading of "To Whom It May Concern (Tell Me Lies About Vietnam)"; Ernst Jandl, who performed ten minutes of sneezing in homage to German modernist Kurt Schwitters; and William Burroughs, who didn't read but played a tape over the Albert Hall PA system.

By January '66, things were moving on the alternative underground scene in the United States. The opening of the Psychedelic Shop in the Haight-Ashbury district of San Francisco reflected a cultural shift in the city, as a huge influx of youth came looking for an alternative universe to the parental home.

This concentration of young hippies attempting to create a new social utopia would produce practical problems and a law-and-order backlash from the local authorities. The Diggers, a local anarchist community, set up shelters for new arrivals, providing twenty-four-hour lodgings and a permanent free lawyer on Haight Street as part of a legal-aid program.

Over on the East Coast, Andy Warhol staged the Exploding Plastic Inevitable for the first time at a dinner for the New York Society for Clinical Psychiatry on January 13, 1966. The event, called "Up-Tight," included performances by the Velvet Underground and Nico, with Gerard Malanga and Edie Sedgwick as dancers, and Jonas Mekas and Barbara Rubin interviewing and filming the psychiatrists. Further shows were held at the Dom in St. Mark's Place, the East Village's hippest nightspot, and moved on to various other North American cities.

Counterculture news from abroad would arrive in London via the underground free press, which offered updates on current activities on both the West and East coast of America. Activities commented and reported on through a growing alternative communication system including the *Los Angeles Free Press*, cited as the first underground newspaper and established in May 1964 by journalist Art Kunkin.

In the autumn of 1965, during my second year of study at the London College of Printing, I worked with George Clark, a founder member of Campaign for Nuclear Disarmament (CND), art-editing the Summer '66 issue of his quarterly magazine *People and Politics*. The issue contained a special supplement highlighting the work of Clark and Rhaune Laslett and the Notting Hill Community Workshop. Clark and Laslett established the first community-action group to fight slum landlords and poor housing conditions in North Kensington, where postwar housing shortages were being exploited by "slum landlords" such as Peter Rachman, and enforcers such as Michael de Freitas, who later became known as Michael X after embracing radical black politics.

Through Clark I met "Hoppy" Hopkins at a meeting to organize the London Free School in Notting Hill Gate in January '66. Hoppy was a Cambridge-educated physics/mathematics scholar and former nuclear physicist, now working as a photojournalist, and a major influence in the developing London counterculture scene. He and Laslett had created the school idea together, and Hoppy asked me to help organize and design a community newspaper called *The Grove* as well as a logo, posters, and paperwork for the various school activities, which included discussion groups and

left: John "Hoppy" Hopkins—*left, in blue jacket*—and demonstrators circling Eros at Piccadilly Circus, London, during a "Legalise Marijuana" happening, January 1967.

opposite: Marchers take part in a CND rally at Trafalgar Square, London, in 1965.

night classes on subjects from housing problems to race relations. The London Free School organized the Notting Hill Fayre, which in time would become the famous Notting Hill Carnival, as well as the All Saints Church Hall school-funding concerts that first introduced Pink Floyd and the psychedelic sound to a developing counterculture.

The *International Times* (later called simply *IT* after objections by the London *Times* newspaper) was the first European alternative newspaper for the counterculture. It was founded by Hopkins alongside Barry Miles, the owner of the Indica alternative bookshop and gallery, and Jim Haynes, founder of Edinburgh's Traverse Theatre in 1963 (with a group of like-minded theater enthusiasts) and the Edinburgh Festival Fringe.

IT was first published on October 14, 1966, and launched at an all-night rave at the Roundhouse in Chalk Farm, London, the following day. Italian actress Monica Vitti, directors Michelangelo Antonioni and Peter Brook, and Paul McCartney were all seen wandering about. There was also a "jelly performance," film screenings, and a cubicle selling fortunes. *IT* was a fortnightly publication affiliated with the Underground Press Syndicate, which supported the free use of shared information—not unlike the modern internet. Fellow members of the syndicate included the *East Village Other*, the *Los Angeles Free Press*, the *Peace News*, the *Berkeley Barb*, and the *Fifth Estate*.

Hoppy invited me to art-edit *IT* toward the end of '66, and I left art college in my third year of study to take up duties on the paper. It was an easy decision. *IT* provided a window into a world of mind-enhancing opinion. As well as design duties, I would report on developments in performance art and gallery happenings. With environmentalist and engineer Graham Stevens, I would interview Buckminster Fuller, the American architect, systems theorist, and inventor of the geodesic dome. Our article, titled "Playing the Game of the Universe," covered a range of topics over a two-hour interview, including the global actions of youth and generational conflicts based on a talk given during free-speech protests at UC Berkeley, as well as civil-rights issues and the Vietnam War. Fuller made it clear that his idea of revolution came in a business suit rather than the divisive look of hippie rebellion.

The *IT* was always short of funds, so Hoppy and Joe Boyd—a record producer and head of Elektra Records' London office—decided to try to establish a regular source of income for the paper by opening a music club using bands who had played to packed audiences at All Saints Church Hall in Notting Hill. Boyd discovered an Irish dancehall called the Blarney Club in the basement of 31 Tottenham Court Road, under the Gala Berkeley Cinema. He negotiated a fee for the overnight Friday/Saturday use of the space, and the UFO Club—as they decided to call it—was launched on the evening of December 23, 1966, with Pink Floyd and Soft Machine as its resident bands.

The launch poster, designed by Michael English and featuring the face of Karen Astley (girlfriend of Pete Townshend), announced the evenings of December 23 and 30 as "Nite Tripper"; soon, UFO—short for both "Unidentified Flying Object" and "Ultimate Freak Out"—became the settled name for the club.

howling wolf meets shepherd's bush
introducing the who
by Richard Barnes

Richard Barnes first met Pete Townshend at Ealing Art College in 1961, and became acquainted with the members of his fledgling band the following year. Here, he recalls his experiences of living with Pete over the next few years, and observing the rise of The Who from close quarters.

first met the band in 1962, when they were The Detours: Roger Daltrey, Pete Townshend, John Entwistle, and drummer Dougie Sandom. It was Roger's band. He'd hated school and been expelled for fighting and smoking. Roger drove the van, carried the gear, and made the decisions. He was determined and hard working.

Everything revolved around the group's Austin 152 van. The passenger door was damaged, so Roger had welded it shut. To get in or out we had to use the driver's door, and Roger had to repeatedly move. It was a "bloody palaver" and also quite dangerous. On the side was a crude circle and an arrow loosely based on the medical "male" symbol, which was the inspiration for The Who's 1964 "Maximum R&B" arrow Marquee poster.

The Detours played mainly covers of current chart songs. Bands were all learning on the job, and week-by-week, gig-by-gig, you could clearly notice The Detours getting better and gaining confidence.

Ealing Art College was an easy-going, enlightened sort of place, and we loved it. The floor below the art school was a school of fashion, with all bar one of the students female. Upstairs was a school of photography. Across the road was a small seedy cafe, Sid's Cafe, catering for the rebels and escapees. We shared Sid's with lorry drivers. Alongside the Top 50 on the jukebox were some obscure blues singles, including "Green Onions" by Booker T., Jimmy Reed's "Bright Lights, Big City," and Slim Harpo's "King Bee." None of them widely known or available outside the United States.

These rare gems were from the record collection of two American photography students, Tom Wright and his friend Cam, who shared a flat opposite the art school. They also had something else not widely available at the time—marijuana. Subsequently, six months later, they both ended up being deported for selling the stuff, and that's when Pete and I inherited their flat—along with their two-hundred-plus album collection.

What an unbelievable gift for a fledgling musician! This collection was like a history of (mostly black) American music: predominantly blues and R&B, but also jazz, soul, rock, folk, swing, and some comedy LPs. We spent untold hours immersed in these albums. We went to bed and woke up to Jimmy Reed.

Art schools could be seen as effete and middle-class. Roger didn't appreciate arriving one evening to find us not ready but lying on mattresses, stoned, engrossed in Elmore James. "Lazy, arty-farty, pot-smoking bastards!" was his considered opinion. Years later Pete admitted, "If Roger had been less forceful, I would have stayed home in my cloud of pot smoke."

Now musically spoilt for choice, Pete's gripes about playing the same "corny" numbers met with resistance, particularly from Doug, who hated the blues. It was Doug, however, who always calmed things down when Pete and Roger argued over musical direction. Several R&B numbers were eventually included, and the band noticeably benefitted. They became much more distinctive and earned some kudos. Roger developed into a pretty convincing blues singer with a sort of "Howling Wolf meets Shepherd's Bush" growl. He also became fairly adept on the harmonica.

Two of the biggest influences on Pete (apart perhaps from the blues collection and smoking pot) came not from the art course itself but from the various visiting lecturers. Artist and activist Gustav

FOX & GOOSE HOTEL
HANGER LANE, EALING W.5

JIVING & TWISTING
FRIDAYS
FEATURING THE DYNAMIC
"DETOURS"
7.30–11.00 P.M.   4/- ADMISSION
LICENSED BALLROOM BAR
BUSES—83, 187 TO DOOR   112, 105 TWO MINUTES   TRAINS—HANGER LANE, PARK ROYAL
COMMENCING **FRIDAY, 11TH JAN.**

top right: A poster for The Detours from 1963. The original of this—one of three similar posters owned by John Entwistle—fetched £18,000 during the John Entwistle Collection sale at Sotheby's London auction rooms in May 2003.

bottom right: The Detours in 1963. *Left to right*: Entwistle, drummer Doug Sandom, Daltrey, and Townshend. Daltrey drove the band's van, which even at this early stage in the group's career was embellished with an arrow—an insignia that was soon to become synonymous with The Who.

Metzger strongly promoted the auto-destructive art movement, and jazz musician Malcolm Cecil swapped his bow for a handsaw and spontaneously sawed through the strings of his double bass during a lecture. Both had a profound effect on Pete.

The band rarely visited our flat. They didn't socialize with each other. One night, however, they all turned up after a gig. John had seen a band on TV with a similar name, Johnny Devlin and the Detours. We sat around thinking up new names. I was surprised at how open-minded the others were, particularly as I was very stoned, so risked appearing a bit "arty-farty." By the early morning, we'd narrowed it down to either Pete's choice: The Hair, or mine: The Who. The next day it was settled when Roger casually grunted to me in passing, "It's The Oo, innit!"

With that, everything changed. The name was daring and stood out. The audiences would—as we'd hoped—do a puzzled double take. Plus, it was so short it looked huge on the posters.

A local Shepherd's Bush businessman invested in the band. They quit jobs and art school, and The Who became a full-time, salaried band. A Fontana Records audition followed. It was going well until the A&R man criticized Doug Sandom's drumming. Then, to our astonishment, Pete joined in, demanding, "Get it together, or get out!" The audition broke up. Pete later explained that he sensed they were losing their big chance, and Doug was holding them back. He was also thirteen or fourteen years older than the others—and it was starting to show.

Doug left the band, and they relied on a session drummer until someone told John, "My mate can play better than your drummer!" So this "mate" with ginger-dyed hair and a ginger-colored suede jacket played on Bo Diddley's "Road Runner." He was loud and broke the drum pedal. It was Keith Moon, who had played in another local band, The Beachcombers. He became The Who's new drummer. The difference was immediate, and we sensed this could be a massive turning point.

Keith himself appeared intimidated at first. Unbelievably, he was quiet and well behaved—almost human. And we sensible heavy blues devotees had to come to terms with his relentless frivolous surfing music.

The next turning point was the hiring of Peter Meaden as publicist. Ace mod Meaden was fascinating, fast-talking, and permanently on purple hearts. Guided by Meaden, the band adopted the mod look with new haircuts and clothes. He had a bit of an uphill struggle, particularly with John, who resented being told what to wear. I found Meaden exciting, and supported his ambitious ideas—apart from the name change. The newly christened High Numbers surprisingly won over this ultra-critical audience, becoming the mods' own band. However, their record, "I'm the Face," didn't win over anyone. It just didn't sell, which left the band with a huge predicament.

Around the time Meaden took over, I started running the Railway Hotel club in Harrow, regularly featuring The Who. We paid them a whopping, eye-watering £20 (around $55 at the time, and almost £400 or $500 today). Their average was about £16. And when The Who became the High Numbers, the Railway followed, transforming from a blues club into a mod club.

Pete and I now had a more spacious flat, and I had a room designated for printing posters. My girlfriend Jan and I, and sometimes Pete, silkscreen-printed High Numbers posters for the Railway. We used to go out after midnight in my partner Lionel's gangster-like silver grey Mark 9 Jaguar and fly-post them illegally on empty shops around the area. It was all very exciting, dodging the police and so on, and it paid off, as the Railway was jam-packed every week. Word was spreading about this band whose members were actual mods.

One night, a bouncer warned that a "posh straight bloke in a suit" was outside. I panicked, as we almost certainly let too many people in, but all my efforts to deny him entry failed. Kit Lambert had been driving past and noticed the row of scooters outside. He was a film director, searching for a pop group for a documentary. The Railway was hot, dark, crowded, and extremely loud, and Lambert said it was like a "version of Hades" when he entered. He knew straightaway this was the band he and his partner Chris Stamp (actor Terence Stamp's "better-looking" brother) had spent six months searching for. In the end, Lambert and Stamp took over complete management of the band, dispensing with Pete Meaden but still continuing with his plans. Sensibly, they changed the name back to The Who.

All attempts to build a recording studio in our flat failed miserably. For months, we'd been hindered by the cumbersome eight-by-four-foot heavy soundproofing insulation sheets we'd ordered but abandoned obstructing the stairs. Eventually, Pete set up his two Vortexion tape machines and equipment in the kitchen. His Heath Robinson setup included a makeshift metronome: a pencil taped to the deck of a variable-speed record turntable, which, with each rotation, brushed against a cardboard marker, making a regular click, so delivering a reliable, fully adjustable, tempo.

I remember his early songs sounding very Jimmy Reed–like. He was very pleased when I said his first version of "I Can't Explain" was like "Bob Dylan with a hint of Mose Allison." When they realized that Lambert's secretary knew the wife of Shel Talmy, who'd recently produced "You Really Got Me," with its powerful guitar riff, for The Kinks, Pete substantially improved his demo, adding his own powerful guitar riff, and they sent it to Talmy.

Talmy subsequently produced "I Can't Explain," which reached #8 in the UK charts—and the rest, I suppose, is history . . .

far left: McInnerney's *Dusk to Dawn* silkscreen poster for the UFO club in London, promoting an event featuring Arthur Brown, Alexis Korner, Tomorrow, and the Bonzo Dog Doo-Dah Band, July 1967.

left: A young woman, partly obscured by the psychedelic light show, dances in front of the stage while Pink Floyd perform at the UFO, December 1966.

opposite: Pete Townshend, surrounded by records and instruments, in the top-floor room of his apartment at 87 Wardour Street, London, late 1966.

Pete and the Ultimate Freak Out

On the night of the UFO club's launch, the same face that appeared on the poster came floating down the wide staircase entrance and up to the ticket desk, which I manned with my girlfriend of the time, Katie Lambert. This was our first introduction to Karen—without Pete, who was performing a gig with The Who that night. She was accompanied by her friends Annie Duprée, Michael English, and Angela Brown, all of whom, along with Pete, attended Ealing Art College in the early sixties.

Michael English left Ealing in the summer of '66 and teamed up with Nigel Waymouth to create the design team Hapshash and the Coloured Coat. Nigel was also co-creator of the clothing boutique Granny Takes a Trip. Hapshash would go on to create many of the iconic posters of the London psychedelic scene. Meanwhile, Karen worked with Angela and Annie at their company, Hem and Fringe, in Pimlico and made shirts with Angela for Michael Rainey's shop Hung on You from Michael and Angela's Princedale Road studio in Holland Park and Karen's flat in Eccleston Square.

A close friendship would grow out of the club and into each other's lives. The UFO was a good place to hang out; we were comfortable in each other's company and felt like a family, sharing interests that included listening to the latest sounds, following the latest developments in fashion, art, and design, and discussing politics and the price and quality of drugs. "It was here we would chat and introduced ourselves for the first time," Karen recalls. "I was at the UFO club from the beginning—it was a lovely place to be on a Friday night, just wandering around observing people."

An early sense of familiarity would expand along with an increasing community of like-minded souls as the audience for the UFO grew. Karen often went to the club with Pete, who would watch men watching Karen dance. I was also fond of watching the UFO congregation, gently wandering and circulating in self-absorbed highs, and sometimes blowing bubbles made from a mixture of soap and water—something I referred to when I created the poster for the 14-Hour Technicolor Dream a few months later.

Hyde Park Happening

I bumped into Pete Townshend again in January '67, at the offices of *International Times*. His interview with Barry Miles was due to appear in issue eight of *IT*, which was my first complete issue as art editor. In the interview, Pete spoke of his admiration for auto-destructive art, recalling attending lectures by its major exponent, Gustav Metzger, at Ealing ("he was my big hero"), and aired his thoughts on wanting to "break through" materialism ("I'm probably the biggest, most stupid materialist in existence"). Asked by Miles if he had a philosophical standpoint, Pete replied bluntly, "No, I don't think I have." That would soon change.

I had helped out on occasion with production of the newspaper during its seven previous issues, when *IT* looked more like a traditional broadsheet newspaper, with headlines, columns of text, and photos—a look defined by the restrictions of letterpress (or relief) printing. Once I became art editor, I made *IT* look less like a newspaper and more like a poster. (This issue also carried an image illustrating an esoteric geometric mandala form, depicting a hippie

The International Times   No 8   Feb 13–26 1967/1s

ginsberg • townshend (who) • snyder • mandrake root

above left: A silkscreen poster by McInnerney advertising the 14 Hour Technicolor Dream, the *IT* benefit event held at Alexandra Palace, London, April 29, 1967.

above right: The "hippie mandala" cover designed by McInnerney for issue 8 of the *International Times* newspaper, dated February 13–26, 1967, which featured Barry Miles's interview with Pete Townshend alongside articles by the poets Allen Ginsberg and Gary Snyder.

opposite left: A 1960 Buick Electra Convertible, as hand-painted by the design team Binder Edwards Vaughan in 1966 and used as the wedding car at the marriage of Mike and Katie McInnerney.

opposite right: The Flying Dragon, the hippie tea house created by OMtentacle design duo of McInnerney and Dudley Edwards at 436 Kings Road, Chelsea, London, as photographed in 1967.

universe with ginseng reference and eastern allusion.) On March 9, 1967, the police attempted to close down *IT*. Funds were required to cover legal costs as a consequence of the raid. The 14-Hour Technicolor Dream, a fundraising event being organized at the Alexandra Palace in North London, became a free-speech benefit. I was briefed to produce the poster. On April 29, 1967, some ten thousand people turned up and tuned in to Europe's first major underground gathering. Pete was listed on the poster to play on the night, but I did not see him in the crowded hall.

We were seeing quite a lot of Karen around this time, often visiting her home in Eccleston Square, and we would chat with Pete when he wasn't out gigging with The Who. Around this time, Katie and I decided to get married. The date was set for Saturday, May 13, 1967, and the place would be London's Hyde Park, after we had done the legal bit at Kensington Register Office. "Hoppy" Hopkins would be best man, and he promoted the event as a "happening" to the press. Karen, a fashion student at Ealing when she first met Pete, designed our wedding outfits, and used her home for fittings. Bride and groom, high on acid, took the wedding party to the bandstand at Kensington Gardens. The bridal vehicle was a hand-painted Buick Electra, provided courtesy of the Binder Edwards Vaughan (BEV) design team, who specialized in psychedelic murals, paintings, furniture, and cars.

After the wedding, Katie and I moved from Denbigh Road to a top-floor apartment in an old Edwardian mansion block on the corner of Shaftesbury Avenue and Bloomsbury Street, on the edge of Covent Garden. We shared the place with Simon Barley, who helped fund the *International Times*. Visitors to the flat would include Pete and Karen, Yoko Ono (who at the time was recruiting people for her short film *Bottoms*), Mick Farren of the rock group Social Deviants, *OZ* magazine art editor Martin Sharp, poets Mike Horovitz and Thom Gunn, musicians Bert Jansch and Al Stewart, and David Bowie, who did a couple of photo shoots on the roof with his manager of the time, Calvin Lee.

I had a studio in the apartment from which I established a freelance design and illustration business, having left *IT* as a consequence of the police raid. One of my first commissions came via Barry Miles, who introduced me to Susan "Pussy" Weber, an heiress, model, actress, and "it-girl" of pre-Raphaelite beauty. She had just accessed a trust fund to lease a retail space at 436 Kings Road, Chelsea. Her plan was to open a hippie teahouse, and Miles had suggested I create a hand-painted, customized shop front for her.

Weber's interest in the *I Ching* (an ancient Chinese text also known as *The Book of Changes*) led to a throwing of Yarrow Stalks to create hexagrams from which readings can be taken. This led to two readings: one related to the Heavenly Dragon and Earthly Dragon that became the exterior theme for the shop, the other to the spirit of the white horse that roams the earth became the subject for the shop interior. Pussy named the shop the Flying Dragon and brought in Barbara Allen as a partner in the venture. I asked Dudley Edwards of BEV to join me in the project and help prepare sketches for the teahouse. Dudley's experience of materials and suppliers for flamboyant paints and knowledge of techniques for painting outdoor objects would prove extremely helpful to the job.

perfect master
the life and teachings of meher baba

Meher Baba's principal message of love was recognized by young seekers at a time when conditions seemed perfect for its reception in the run-up to the Summer of Love. It was a message given extra weight and meaning by the life of a Perfect Master devoted to merging inner truth and external actions in the service of humanity as a whole.

Meher Baba was born in February 24, 1894, as Merwan Sheriar Irani to Persian Zoroastrian parents (Zoroastrianism, or Mazdayasna, being one of the world's oldest active religions). His mission as Avatar—the Hindu word for Godman—began in 1921 and followed his early illumination and spiritual transformation at the age of nineteen, in 1913, when he was blessed with a kiss and enlightened by *Perfect Master* Hazrat Babajan under her favored neem tree.

Over time, Meher Baba developed practical examples of his principal message of love. He worked with disciples (*mandali*) in India, establishing, in 1923, an ashram outside Ahmednagar, which he named Meherabad. Here, he worked with the poor through free schools, dispensaries, and shelters, which were open to all castes and faiths. He traveled extensively, working with spiritual aspirants called *masts* —those who had become "intoxicated" with God—and distributed grain, cloth, and money to the destitute. His life was devoted not to teaching but to awakening humanity to the unifying messages of love as truth given by great messengers of the past including Zoroaster, Jesus, Buddha, Muhammad, and Krishna. His belief that all had been said was given emphasis by the vow of silence he made on July 10, 1925, and observed for forty-three years till his death in 1969.

Baba made first contact with the West in 1931, traveling over to England on the SS *Rajputana*—the same ship that carried Mahatma Gandhi to the second Round Table Conference on the Indian constitution. The two men met several times on board. During those meetings, Baba advised Gandhi, as an advanced soul, to concentrate on his work with God and leave politics. In Britain, Baba met and established a base for his work through Delia De Leon and Charles Purdom, a journalist and editor of *Everyman* magazine. Having connected with disciples in Europe, he visited America in 1932, establishing a center at Myrtle Beach, South Carolina, and becoming a celebrity visitor to Hollywood, meeting with Gary Cooper, Tallulah Bankhead, Ernst Lubitsch, and others. Mary Pickford and Douglas Fairbanks Jr. held a reception in his honor at their house in Beverly Hills, *Pickfair*, where he spoke of his great love of movies and his belief that they were the most important vehicle for exploring ideas of truth in modern times.

Baba's *Discourses* contains the most complete example of his teachings, offering a carefully structured manual for the seeker on a spiritual journey. Its chapters cover many subjects, including the human search for Truth and God, spiritual advancement, and discipleship. For me, the chapter on love provided the most holistic sense of being in the world, making real the idea that everything is connected and that I could recognize this and understand it.

In nineteen themed paragraphs, Baba describes love as the force that binds everything. Gravity, to which all planets and stars are subject, is in its way a dim reflection of the love that pervades all things in the universe. Love reigns in inanimate nature through forces of cohesion and affinity. The object of love sustains the animal kingdom, and through instinct it feeds both the body and desire to reproduce. Human love through self-conscious knowledge has to adjust to reason and complex levels of expression from lust, infatuation, greed, power, anger, to jealousy, and to understand tolerance, the search for good and grace in others. The journey into divine love becomes a personal relationship between a disciple and

above left: A 1967 paperback edition of Meher Baba's *Discourses*. First published in 1939, it is considered, alongside *God Speaks*, one of his most important works.

above right: A portrait of Baba in his early twenties, taken shortly after he began his spiritual transformation.

master as experience moves beyond illusion and individual ego to an original unity of being.

Discourses outlines *sanskaras*, or mental impressions, and their formation and function as a concept in the karma theory of Indian philosophies. It describes how all that we experience through the senses gathers as *sanskaras*, and how these are the very things that can define us as well as the very things that will also bind us. The hard business of a spiritual journey is about managing illusion created by *sanskaras* and leaving them behind as we begin to see what is real.

Baba's chapter on ego and its termination is such a hard hill to climb that it requires three subchapters to outline its function in the spiritual process. Ego is formed by the inherent nature of living beings to store, integrate, and evaluate experience around the self. Ego can take over a sense of "I" and start considering itself the central identity of the individual. This can hinder self-consciousness, becoming ever more difficult to proceed unless it can be weakened.

The subject of *Maya* is so tricky it needs four subchapters to provide a guide to the topic. *Maya* is the creator of illusion. It is not false, not unreal, and not duality, but it gives false impressions, makes the unreal appear real, and is the *cause* of duality. Baba states that it is necessary for the seeker to know what is false, to know it to be false, and to get rid of the false by knowing it to be false.

Many more chapters and subjects contained in *Discourses* provide a rich platform of knowledge, on the understanding that at some point, help is required to create the right disciple/master relationship to enable the journey of the seeker. This all chimed perfectly with the spirit of 1967, so I mentioned it when Pete and I first discussed Baba at my studio in Shaftesbury Avenue.

> What was so sneaky about the whole affair was the way Baba crept into my life. At first his words were encouraging, his state of consciousness and his claims to be the Christ exciting and daring, later they became scary. It became clear that the party was over."

Pete Townshend, "In Love with Meher Baba," *Rolling Stone*, November 26, 1970

Seekers

One day, Dudley came to the studio at Shaftesbury Avenue after returning from a trip to Bradford with Martin and Chris Cook to visit Mary Parry, a long-term follower of the Indian spiritualist master Meher Baba. Dudley had with him some books by Baba, which we began to read, and, as we did so, we began to recognize something deep and familiar.

Mary had mentioned that Baba meetings were held at the Poetry Society in Earls Court, so one day Dudley and I decided to go along, with Chris and Martin, to see for ourselves. (Dudley asked Paul McCartney to come along, too, but George Harrison had arranged a meeting with the Maharishi on the same day.) We made it to the Poetry Society and entered through huge doors of the large room where the meeting was to be held. We expected a packed meeting, but instead we found a small group of four people in a circle of chairs, lost in the space of the room. The group comprised actress and Q Theatre co-founder Delia de Leon, treasurer Joyce Bird, and journalist Tom Hopkinson and his wife Dorothy. Delia, Tom, and Dorothy had been devotees of Baba for many years, Delia since 1931. I was moved by their long-lived love for Baba and their enduring belief and faith in him. As is the way with Baba, it is through the actions of others that you glimpse his principal message of love. Delia's slightly anxious air of care and Tom's strong ethical and moral qualities were testament to this.

It took a while for us to fully appreciate what we had come across, however. The Poetry Society meeting had little immediate impact, but luckily Delia had taken our contact information and remained in touch.

Soon after, she invited us to her flat in Kew for tea, sandwiches, and Baba anecdotes, offering us further reading material that extended our awareness as we became more entranced by Baba's life and truth. We were taken by Delia's sheer joy at describing Baba; how she felt in his presence, and how, as she watched him interact with others, she could see God at work.

Because of Delia's background in theater, she had an acute awareness of the behavior of others, which made her particularly astute at reading the human dynamics of aspirants and seekers in the presence of Baba. She talked about his robust love for each of them, about the kinetic nature of his work with individuals, and his "big hugs."

There is no typical Baba lover; each appears very different, unique and complicated, like any other human being, and he would customize his responses accordingly, sometimes playfully, sometimes impishly, sometimes in a controlling manner. Sometimes he lit a slow fuse with a lesson that seemed obscure at the time it was delivered but would later reveal itself to the aspirant at the right moment in time. Like a film director working closely with an actor, he would obtain the best interpretation and *performance* from those who came to him. His actions were intimate yet could be seen to benefit the overall nature of an unfolding narrative that only he understood at the time. He offered no simple solution to the daily business of dealing with the self other than to not worry and be happy and to love him—all of which initially sounds simple, but in fact goes very deep. Many would speak of feeling ecstatic and emotional, even collapsing in tears when meeting him.

"MIRACLE MAN" TALKS TO "DAILY MIRROR"

Indian Mystic's Finger Signals to Preserve Seven Years' Silence

HIS MESSAGE TO THE WORLD

Waiting for Spirit to Move Him to Revelation—Miracles Performed "If Necessary"

Shri Meher Baba, the Indian mystic, who claims to be another Messiah and capable of performing miracles, talked on his alphabet-board with the *Daily Mirror* in London yesterday during an exclusive interview.

He has come to England to join a little community of devotees at Combe Martin in Devonshire, and during the interview preserved his seven years' silence by a system of finger signals.

"I can perform miracles if necessary," he said, and added that miracles were unimportant and "child's play to anyone who has reached my state of consciousness."

Baba is expected to give a message to the world when he goes to America. "He is waiting for the spirit to move him to a revelation," said one of his disciples.

TO LEAD WESTERN WORLD

Shri Meher Baba on Reasons for His Visit to England

BY A SPECIAL CORRESPONDENT

"The statement that I am a 'Messiah' is not to be taken in a literal sense," Shri Meher Baba, the new Indian religious teacher, told me yesterday.

Shri Meher Baba was seated in his apartment in West London, surrounded by five faithful disciples who are travelling with him. His slight figure was wrapped in a simple white robe, emphasising his mane of dark hair and heavy eyebrows and moustache.

THE MOVING FINGERS

He has a gentle, affectionate manner and welcomed me with a graceful inclination. His large, lustrous, black eyes, very observant, lit up with a pleasant expression as his thin brown finger moved swiftly across an alphabet board on his knee.

The interview had started. Meher Baba, who has been claimed as a new Messiah, was trying to speak to me through the veil of his self-imposed silence of seven years.

One of his disciples turned to me and said: "Baba says that you are good. . . . He is pleased to meet you."

What was his message for the English people? I wanted to know. And very swiftly the finger moved again. He was spelling in English, but with short cuts and abbreviations that only the swift and practised eyes of his disciples could follow.

The Western world, Baba thought, tended to concentrate too much upon materialism. Materialism was not an altogether bad feature of Western life. It was, indeed, valuable in the development of our lives.

But he wished to lead the West towards spiritual truths, without Churches or creeds, to a realisation of the possibilities of the spirit that might become a part of our everyday life.

BABA'S REVELATION

Asked when he would be able to give his message publicly to the world, Baba told me that he would be going within a month to America, where it was possible that within two or three months' time he might break his silence.

I was told by a disciple that Baba did not make any vow to keep silent for seven years. "He just entered into the silence, and when the time comes, sooner or later, he will speak." He is waiting for the spirit to move him to his revelation.

Meanwhile, he is giving counsel to those who seek it. He will go within a week to Devon, where he will be welcomed at the Ashram, near Combe Martin.

"What do you teach your inquirers?" I asked.

"According to their individual needs. But when I speak to the whole world, then my teaching will be universal."

Asked if it were true that he would perform miracles, Meher Baba replied, "If necessary." But he did not think that he would perform miracles in England . . . perhaps in America it might happen.

One of the disciples explained that Baba did not perform miracles "to order."

Baba made further signals, describing how he had performed miracles in India. He had bathed lepers and they had been cured; he had cured people of contagious diseases.

"Can you raise the dead?" I asked.

"If necessary," replied Baba. But he did not know why I was so insistent on miracles. Miracles, he explained, were really unimportant. One who had passed into his high spiritual sphere had travelled beyond the earthly manifestations that one associated with miracles.

"Christ raised the dead and made the blind to see," he explained, "but to anybody who has attained the state of consciousness that I have reached miracles are child's play."

He conveyed that the attainment of a spiritual unity with the non-material world was something far greater than any outward sign that he might make.

The beginning of Meher Baba's religious experience is traced to his meeting with an Indian saint, Baba Jan. I asked if she had taught him all he is teaching now.

THE DOOR UNLOCKED

"No, she did not teach me exactly," replied Baba. "She unlocked the door. I knew that I had powers within me, but it was she who showed me what they meant. It was not something to be taught, but to be lived and experienced."

I asked if he imposed any discipline or rule of life on his followers. Did he encourage fasting, or vegetarianism?

"Only according to their individual needs. One of my disciples in India has lived for four years on water and a little milk.

He said that he had no interest in the political affairs of India, and asked me to correct the statement that he was the spiritual adviser of Gandhi.

TALK WITH GANDHI

"Gandhi met me on the liner Rajputana and we talked of spiritual experiences. Gandhi was interested, and said that he would like to meet me in America. I said that he could come to me after he had finished with his political work," was Baba's explanation.

"You mean that you do not think politics and the spiritual life have much to do with each other?"

"Not directly," replied Baba. "But eventually, of course, the spiritual experience becomes universal and includes the political affairs of the world."

He wanted all the nations to be brought together, but he did not wish to work for India alone.

A disciple informed me that Baba has "many thousands of followers in India. It is impossible to say how many. They are chiefly round about Bombay and many are in the Madras Presidency."

FAITH IN MIRACLES

Meher Baba thought it was unlikely that he would hold any public meeting in England, but it would depend upon circumstances. He had addressed a large gathering—by means of his alphabet-board—during the voyage on the liner.

He showed me correspondence from America, indicating that his visit to the United States is being preceded by a wave of publicity through the American Press.

A disciple showed me a copy of a letter from a woman devotee to the Countess Tolstoy, in which it was stated that Meher Baba had miraculously cured her of a tumour. I was told that such miracles are a matter of faith in Baba's teaching.

"From which religious teacher do you derive your philosophy?" I asked. "From Christ? . . . Buddha?"

"From no one teacher in particular," Baba replied. "Christ, Buddha, Krishna . . . these are names for states of consciousness. . . ."

"And you have studied them all?"

Shri Meher Baba nodded and smiled.

above left: "Miracle Man": the *Daily Mirror* newspaper's account of Meher Baba's visit to London in April 1932. "Can you raise the dead?" the *Mirror*'s reporter asked, to which Baba replied, "If necessary."

above right: Baba and Delia de Leon in St Mark's Square, Venice, during Baba's European tour of 1932.

above: Pete Townshend in his home studio in
Twickenham in 1970. A portrait of Meher Baba
is visible on the wall behind him.

"Waffling On"

It was at my Shaftesbury Avenue apartment that I first spoke with Pete about Baba. I was hosting a party for the Dutch couple Simon and Marijke, who were part of the psychedelic art and design team known as The Fool. They were in London working on various projects for The Beatles at the time. At one point during the course of the evening, Pete and I were in my studio, looking at sketches in progress for the Flying Dragon teahouse. The conversation turned to the *I Ching*, as I discussed the Flying Dragon project with him. Pete knew of *I Ching* and its function as a divination text and as an aid to making decisions based on the random throwing of sticks or coins. (John Cage, Hermann Hesse, and Philip K. Dick, among others, were influenced by this text. Hesse himself was popular on the underground scene of the time, and Pete had read him and referenced him in our chat.)

In his book *Who I Am*, Pete writes about "waffling on" during our first discussion of Baba. I considered it more that we were exploring each other's understanding of being in the world. (It may be a cliché that men enjoy talking to each other more about abstract ideas than anything too personal, but I think therein lies an element of truth. We reveal ourselves through our interests—what we believe or which notions we support.)

Pete had recently returned from performing at the Monterey Pop Festival in June 1967. The flight back from the United States was a bit higher and scarier than he'd expected, having taken LSD and experienced an out-of-body moment in the cabin of the aircraft. Like myself and others at the time, he considered psychotropic drugs as an aid to some kind of spiritual understanding. (Taking drugs was not a way to be "off your head," nor was it a way to "take leave of your senses," but rather a way to enhance the senses.) I remember long evenings in the safe spaces of friends' apartments, exploring the idea that we are all of one consciousness that is experienced subjectively; that matter is energy condensed into a vibration, that life is a dream and we are what we imagine. The next morning we might all get up and argue about who does the washing up, but at least the apartment, and especially the toilets, would be tidy, unlike in the aftermath of a booze party.

Baba was to make it very clear that drugs would only ever offer mere entertainment—a serious distraction from the real purpose and effort of the true spiritual journey of an individual. It might have been that Pete and I talked that night about the ego and the need of master-aspirant relationships to manage it—an issue that would become part of the *Tommy* story.

Pete loved conversation, and so did I—especially the kind that would roam across and wander around as new subjects developed. A lot of the time, he would work in solitude in the cramped environment of the studio at his home on the Embankment at Twickenham. The studio where he produced demos and experimental recordings was in a small anteroom above the narrow kitchen extension at the back of the house. Conversations with others would provide necessary input and feedback as work progressed on *Tommy*.

The conversation that evening started without any real destination, but it ended up in Baba territory, as though all roads had led there.

something in the air
the world outside

The thirteen months that passed from January '68, when I first heard about Pete's opera idea, to February '69, when we sat in the kitchen of his house with completed artwork, discussing a way to place Meher Baba on the cover, were a time of epochal change. The early optimism and utopian ideas of a developing counterculture expressed in the 1967 Summer of Love gave way to a new realism.

The year 1968 would see a groundswell of frustration against entrenched establishments in the United States, Britain, and across the globe, expressing itself with force on the streets of major towns and cities. The UFO club had disappeared in the previous year, and Joe Boyd's publishing and distribution company, Osiris Visions, which created most of the famous psychedelic posters, ceased to trade at the end of 1968. (Similarly, and with some bitterness, Jim Haynes would be forced to close the Drury Lane Arts Lab in October 1969, having received no support from the Arts Council.)

There was a sense that this was the generation that might have the power to influence change from outside government, as countercultural values of feminism, human rights, the environment, and antiwar sentiment became ideas that would turn into direct action. Happenings gave way to demonstrations on the streets of London, with anti-Vietnam marches and demonstrations, including the 1968 "Battle of Grosvenor Square," and coordinated occupations by the London Squatters Campaign set up in November 1968. Further divisions and disruptions were created in Britain by politician Enoch Powell's "Rivers of Blood" speech of April 1968—a speech that helped legitimize anti-immigration sentiment.

A demonstration held in London in October 1967 and organized by the Vietnam Solidarity Campaign was effectively the start of the mass movement against the Vietnam War in Britain. Around ten thousand people assembled in Trafalgar Square and marched on the US Embassy in Grosvenor Square. Demonstrators were encouraged to resist expected police violence, and scuffles followed when protestors broke through police lines. On March 17, 1968, I was among thirty thousand others who marched from Trafalgar Square to Grosvenor Square to demonstrate at the steps of the US Embassy. What was meant to be a peaceful march descended into a level of disturbance and violence that took us all by surprise. The rumor was that anarchists with a different agenda planned to get into the embassy. Some had come armed with smoke bombs and marbles to unseat the mounted police. There were three hundred arrests. The much larger demonstration that would be called the "Battle of Grosvenor Square" on October 27, 1968, had been hyped by the British press as a possible repetition of recent uprisings in Paris and fighting in Berlin. A petition bearing seventy-five thousand names was handed in at 10 Downing Street.

The killing of Che Guevara by US forces in Bolivia on October 9, 1967, had a further radicalizing effect on young people. The International Marxists Group (IMG), with its focus on the communist revolutions in Cuba and Vietnam, and its contacts through the Fourth International and Bertrand Russell Peace Foundation engagement with the struggle in Bolivia, was in a position to tap into a growing movement seeking revolutionary change. Vietnam Solidarity Campaign (VSC) protests were more attractive to the rising student radicalism of 1968 because they had a more militant and confrontational tone, and were led by figures with fewer connections to the establishment.

In the United States, demonstrations against the war in Vietnam increased throughout 1968, even as newly elected president Richard Nixon promised an end to the conflict. Student protests erupted on the campuses of Columbia University in New York, the University of California in Berkeley, and at Kent State, among others. A variety

of issues prompted the outbreak of unrest, including institutional support for US involvement in the war and the alleged construction of a segregated gymnasium at Columbia University; a call for free speech on campus at UC Berkeley; and protests against police recruiters appearing on campus at Kent State in the autumn of '68. (Ongoing campus unrest at the latter would culminate in the fatal shooting of four unarmed college students by the National Guard on May 4, 1970, after students protested the expansion of the Vietnam war into Cambodia.)

Students would continue their involvement in protest politics in a variety of forms, including forming communes and creating urban social organizations. Several members of the Columbia Students for a Democratic Society group combined with the New York Black Panther Party to create the Weathermen, a group dedicated to the violent overthrow of government. On April 4, 1968, Martin Luther King, Jr. was shot and killed at the Lorraine Motel in Memphis, Tennessee. A prominent leader of the civil rights movement and Nobel Peace Prize laureate, he was famous for his advocacy for nonviolence and civil disobedience in the struggle for equal rights. For some, his death meant the end of the nonviolence strategy. Riots erupted in Detroit on April 4 and 5, and required the deployment of the National Guard. Riots erupted simultaneously in 110 other cities, including Washington, D.C. A month later, on June 6, presidential candidate Robert Kennedy died a day after being shot after celebrating victory in the California primary. His death left a vacuum in the Democratic Party for those championing affordable housing, Medicare, and ending the war in Vietnam. The split in the party

ultimately led to the rise of Nixon and the steady poisoning of politics, and a general feeling of decline in utopian ideals, ethics, and hope.

Four days and nights of violence occurred in the streets of Chicago in the vicinity of the 1968 Democratic National Convention, when ten thousand protesters against the Vietnam War confronted Mayor Daley and the Chicago Police. A global television audience watched as the Chicago police fought protestors on August 28. The "Chicago 8"—protesters Abbie Hoffman, Tom Hayden, David Dellinger, Rennie Davis, John Froines, Jerry Rubin, Lee Weiner, and Bobby Seale—faced trial charges of conspiracy and incitement to riot in connection with the violence in Chicago. None were found guilty of conspiracy; all other charges would be dropped.

In Northern Ireland, the minority Catholic community of Belfast formed a civil rights movement in January 1967, calling for an end to discrimination in the area of voting rights, employment, and housing. The movement drew inspiration from the campaign for equal rights led by Martin Luther King in the United States. Protestants, through the Ulster Unionist Party UUP, had held power since the creation of Northern Ireland in 1921, with policies that marginalized and discriminated against the Catholic minority. The first Catholic civil-rights march took place in Derry on October 5, 1968, with a countermarch by protestants. The province soon descended into violence. After further clashes in August '69, the Northern Ireland government at Stormont requested British troops be sent to restore order. It would be thirty years before a peace process could begin.

The events of May '68 in France further reflected a period of civil unrest, demonstrations, and strikes that brought together student

> " The hippies never expected this kind of violence from the Angels and had no idea what to do about it. The Angels, on the other hand, were quite aware that they were badly outnumbered and knew they could only hope to rule through intimidation."
>
> Joel Selvin, *Altamont: The Rolling Stones, the Hells Angels, and the Inside Story of Rock's Darkest Day*, 2016

concerns about education reforms and issues related to values, order, and entrenched traditions and institutions. Disturbances spread to factories, and strikes involving eleven million workers looking for better wages and working conditions took place. The "Night of the Barricades" on May 10–11 saw pitched battle between protestors using cobblestones against the notorious riot police. Slogans such as "The beach lies beneath the paving stones" and "Banning is banned" were influenced by Situationist International texts in books such as *The Society of the Spectacle* by Guy Debord, which itself influenced ideas, quotes, phrases, and slogans of the insurrections and the protest artistic movement in song, graffiti, and posters. President Charles de Gaulle fled France briefly and after returning called for new elections, which he won. His new, stronger mandate killed the protests.

The German student movement that grew out of street clashes in Berlin during the Shah of Iran's visit in 1967 and the attempted assassination during Easter '68 of Rudi Dutschke of the Socialist German Student League, led to a nationwide attempt by students to block delivery of Axel Springer's tabloid paper *Bild-Zeitung*, who named Dutschke a "public enemy." During the actions, four hundred students were injured, and two died. In May, the revolt reached its climax, with eighty thousand demonstrating at the Bundestag in Bonn against the passing of "German Emergency Acts" allowing the government to limit civil rights, restrict movement, and limit privacy in the case of an emergency. A minority of the New Left that grew out of student social activism would go on to found clandestine revolutionary organizations practicing violent direct action, including the Red Army Faction (Baader-Meinhof Gang) in West Germany.

Helter Skelter

In 1969, recently inaugurated US president Richard Nixon announced a new policy of "Vietnamization" as a way to handover responsibility for the progress of the Vietnam War to the South Vietnamese. This would allow for a planned reduction in US troops in Vietnam to between fifty and seventy thousand in 1969, with further withdrawals in 1970. Operation Keystone Eagle saw the first withdrawals, on June 29, of the 3rd Anti-Tank Battalion, with subsequent withdrawals through July to August 30. (The 1st and 3rd Battalions of the 9th Marines would return to South Vietnam in 1972 during the Easter Offensive, and in April '75 for the final evacuation of American civilians and at-risk Vietnamese.)

A police raid in the early morning hours of June 28, 1969, at the Stonewall Inn in Greenwich Village, New York City, led to the "Stonewall Uprising" demonstrations by members of the gay community, a landmark event in the lead-up to the gay liberation movement. The history of antagonism toward homosexuals in Western society is long and deep, with repressive legislation in both Britain and the United States. Gay Americans in the fifties and sixties faced an aggressive anti-gay legal system—a system that encouraged routine police raids on gay bars and led to feelings of persecution. The Stonewall Inn, at the time owned by the mafia, catered for a range of patrons, including the poorest and most marginalized people in the gay community, drag queens, transgender people, gay men, lesbians, male prostitutes, and homeless youth. After June 28, the police lost control of the situation at Stonewall as residents in Greenwich Village quickly organized into activist groups, concentrating

right: Hells Angels armed with pool cues on the attack during the Altamont Speedway Free Festival near Livermore, California, December 6, 1969. The event would later be described by *Rolling Stone* magazine as "rock and roll's all-time worst day . . . a day when everything went perfectly wrong."

on confrontational tactics; this led directly to the first coordinated gay pride marches in New York City, Los Angeles, and San Francisco on June 28, 1970.

In an era known for peace and love, the murders staged by the Manson Family came as a profound shock. On August 8–9, 1969, four members of the "family" invaded the home of the actress Sharon Tate, wife of the actor and film director Roman Polanski on Cielo Drive, Los Angeles. Tex Watson, under the direction of Charles Manson, carried out the murder of Tate, who was eight and a half months pregnant at the time, as well as three of Tate's friends and a visitor; Polanski was away filming. Terry Melcher, a record producer and previous occupant of the house, had recently snubbed would-be musician Manson, which left Manson disgruntled. Manson instructed Watson to kill the occupants of the house in the most gruesome way possible. Unfortunately, it was Tate and her friends who were at the house on the night of the murders.

In the months leading up to the incident, Manson often spoke to members of his Family about the Beatles song "Helter Skelter," written by Paul McCartney and considered by Manson to be a vision of an apocalyptic war arising from racial tensions between blacks and whites. The "Helter Skelter" scenario was used by the court during Manson's appeal after he and his followers were convicted of the murders. There is something strange about pop-culture's enduring

obsession with Manson, and a grim irony in the fact that he ended up on the cover of *Rolling Stone* magazine, like the rock star he always dreamed of becoming.

The free concert at Altamont closed the decade of the sixties on December 6, 1969, with an event best known for its violence. The day of the concert would include the stabbing to death of Meredith Hunter, two accidental deaths caused by a hit-and-run car accident, and another death caused by LSD-induced drowning. Scores were injured, and there was extensive property damage. The Rolling Stones took to the stage as the final act of the day, with the Hells Angels motorcycle club providing security around the low stage. There was some confusion as to the Angels' role on the day, whether they were policing the event or simply protecting the stage generators. Witness reports describe them behaving with an uncaring attitude, with fistfights breaking out between crowd and Angels by the time the Rolling Stones took to the stage. It was during the Stones' performance of "Under My Thumb" that Angel Alan Passaro drew his knife and stabbed Hunter twice, thinking he had a gun. Altamont has perhaps unfairly become a symbol for the death of the Woodstock Nation. The Stones' Keith Richards was relatively sanguine about the show itself, calling it "basically well-handled, but lots of people were tired and a few tempers got frayed" and "on the whole, a good concert."

So says Dudley Edwards, who was in the studio with us. "I recall at the time Pete was somewhat obsessed by UFOs and extraterrestrial beings, but every time he came up with some philosophical theories, Mike would make the same point from a Baba perspective. Pete, like Mike, had a very inquisitive and questioning mind, and he recognized the importance and substance of Baba's words."

The conversation would touch on a wide range of loosely connected esoteric subject matter, a bit of Eastern thought, a scrap of Western philosophy, and hints of Pete's extraterrestrial conspiracy theory. Many notions I had held about the world felt unconnected— fragments of knowledge coming from separate and distinct territories of experience. Subjects such as art, science, psychology, and philosophy felt like countries on a map with difficult, hard-to-access borders between them. I felt strongly that everything in life is connected, and that the point is to know it and understand it, and for me the spiritual teachings of Baba opened those borders and provided glue to piece things together.

Pete gave his take on the conversation in an interview with *Rolling Stone* in 1970. "I was ranting and raving about, talking too much, and finding in Mike someone who talked just as much as I did. Every time I came up with a world-wise theory that had taken me years of thought to get clear, he would say, 'That's such a coincidence, man, this guy Meher Baba said something similar to that in this book, *The God-Man*.' After I had heard my very last precious revelation hit the dust at the sound of Mike's voice declaring that Baba had already said it I just had to look at the book. What I saw, apart from a photo on the front cover of a strange and elderly man, was shattering."

Deaf, Dumb, and Blind Boy

In October 1967, Katie and I moved from Shaftesbury Avenue to an apartment at Cavendish Court in Cardigan Road on Richmond Hill, which became a small outpost of central London counterculture in the autumn of '67. Our three-bedroom home had a large, open-plan, L-shaped living room/kitchen space, which would provide a venue for Baba meetings as group numbers increased. The living room also doubled as a studio for OMtentacle, a new design partnership between Dudley and myself with Michael Hasted, who we brought in as agent. OMtentacle projects at that time included ongoing work at the Flying Dragon; a poster brief from John Esam, editor of *Image* magazine, for the *La fenêtre rose* psychedelic concert in Paris; and a poster brief from Osiris for a Jazz at The Roundhouse concert in London.

We settled in Richmond because Delia de Leon lived at Kew; by now, we were visiting her on a regular basis, and we liked the idea of being near her. Richmond also had connections with Baba, who had visited the Italian Gothic–styled Star and Garter Hotel (renamed the Petersham Hotel) on Richmond Hill in 1934 when he came to see Delia and her family. And Richmond had for hundreds of years been an Arcadian haunt of poets, artists, and writers, offering the finest picturesque views of the River Thames—a view so precious that it was protected by an act of parliament.

Pete and Karen, meanwhile, were living together in a shared apartment on Ebury Street in Belgravia, and on occasion the four of us would run around town in Pete's spacious 1963 Lincoln Continental Convertible, or sometimes squeeze into my 1958 Ford Popular for a drive. Pete took pleasure in the cars he bought, but it

above left: *Legalise Pot Rally*: a silkscreen poster designed by McInnerney, announcing a demonstration at Speakers' Corner in Hyde Park, London, July 1967.

above right: *Jazz at the Roundhouse*: a lithographic poster advertising a concert at the Roundhouse, London, in 1967, created by the OMtentacle design duo of McInnerney and Dudley Edwards.

never got out of hand. He had a strong sensible streak, inherited from his dad. He told me during a drive how his father had advised him to place the money from his first hit record into property, as security for when the rock and roll died. It was advice that stuck, and it continued down the years.

There was a moment in January '68, while we were hanging out in the kitchen of the Ebury Street flat, when a casual conversation began regarding a project Pete was developing about a deaf, dumb, and blind boy—a collection of songs with a linked story. He was interested in developing musical interests into more ambitious and commercially successful music projects. Recent experiences in California had given him an awareness of a new kind of audience with a growing interest in a search for spiritual experience, very different from a Who performance serving young men. These thoughts about the audience would play an important part in Pete's musical ideas, and through discussions would inform both the music and the album artwork for *Tommy* over the coming months. He outlined bits and pieces of thought in the kitchen, and we discussed the subject of senses and my interest in perception, which I had held since my college days.

Pete found a kindred spirit in Ronnie Lane during a subsequent Australian tour with the Small Faces. Ronnie was the first friend who listened to his interest in Meher Baba without sniggering. Pete at the time was a little reticent about diving into the Baba community, but like me was very taken with the "Baba people" we met at that time and the deep feeling of connection we felt for them. Pete must have sounded like the real thing when chatting with Ronnie, because soon

Ronnie started attending group meetings with Susie, his wife, at Cavendish Court. The gradual migration of some of the early Baba group to Richmond and Twickenham would create a close group of interested seekers and a close neighborhood of friends at some distance from the upheavals of 1968.

Eel Pie and Beyond

An alternative world of spiritual interest was evolving at the same time as the Meher Baba group grew. Our gatherings became more organized, more regular, and larger. Other attendees, alongside myself, Kate, Pete, Karen, and the Lanes, included songwriter and singer Billy Nicholls, Dudley Edwards, Martin and Christine Cook, Pussy Weber, Barbara Allen, Australian artist and musician Vytas Serelis and his wife, and the poet John Horder, among others. The group would listen to Baba teachings from Delia, show films, and read passages from his writings.

In the spring of '68, Katie and I moved into an apartment that was part of a Victorian villa called Willoughby House in Willoughby Road, on the Twickenham side of Richmond Bridge, which spanned the River Thames. Entry to the apartment was through a half-acre garden into the music room, which became our living room; this and the garden would provide another useful space for Baba meetings and events. A neighborhood of friendship grew as Ronnie and Susie Lane settled across the road, followed by Barbara Allen and her partner, Michael Morice.

After their wedding on May 20, Pete and Karen Townshend moved into a beautiful Georgian House in Twickenham facing Eel Pie Island,

One of the dearest women alive is Baba's constant reflection at the London center, Miss Delia de Leon. She is an actress who is now in her seventies, who met Baba when he looked like the most exciting thing to hit Hollywood. 'He was magnificent!' It was clearly love with a capital L at first sight."

Pete Townshend, "In Love with Meher Baba," *Rolling Stone*, November 26, 1970

left: Pete Townshend with Dr. Allan Cohen during a speaking tour of the United Kingdom, as organized by the London Meher Baba Association.

> ❝ All so-called spiritual experiences generated by taking 'mind-changing' drugs such as LSD, mescaline, and psilocybin are superficial and add enormously to one's addiction to the deceptions of illusion which is but the shadow of Reality. No drug, whatever its great promise, can help one to attain the spiritual goal.❞
>
> Meher Baba, *God in a Pill?*, 1966

a short walk along the Thames towpath. Dudley Edwards found lodgings in a large rambling basement apartment in a villa on Riverdale Road. Ronnie Wood would buy the Richmond Hill house belonging to actor John Mills and move in with his partner, Chrissie. Ian "Mac" McLagan, keyboard player with the Small Faces, would move to the area with his wife Sandy after the formation of The Faces. Even Rod Stewart would appear at Marble Hill Park for occasional games of football.

The apartment became a drop-in center and office for a developing local scene and growing Baba activities. Numerous evenings were spent socializing, listening to music, talking about Baba, and popping into each other's homes. Our doors were always open, and socializing was easy and comfortable. It was a perfect little idyll. Willoughby sometimes provided overnight emergency shelter for young homeless people brought to us by the Reverend Ken Leech. (Delia de Leon had introduced us to Ken, the curate at St Anne's Church Soho, who ran the Soho Drug Group. On December 19, 1969, he founded the Centrepoint charity in his Soho church as a shelter for young homeless people in London.)

There were developing contacts with Baba groups in the United States. The Meher Spiritual Center at Myrtle Beach, South Carolina, had been set up by Baba and the actors Elizabeth Patterson and Princess Norina Matchabelli in the 1940s as a retreat for rest, meditation, and renewal of the spiritual life. Sufism Reoriented is a school of spiritual training with its headquarters in Walnut Creek, California, established by Baba in 1952. Ivy Oneita Duce was the living Murshida of the Sufi Order at the time. In 1966, Sufism

Reoriented published *God in a Pill*, in which academics Dr. Allan Cohen, Robert Dreyfuss, and Richard Alpert outline Baba's concern about the effect of drugs on the true spiritual path.

Pete wrote his first plan for *Tommy* in California in February '68, while The Who toured the United States. While in the Bay Area, Pete met with his friend, Rick Chapman, who ran a Baba information center in Berkeley. Pete was impressed with all the Baba lovers he met—people who had lived hard and were now committed to following Baba. These encounters offered him the chance to share his thoughts and developing ideas for *Tommy*, as he did when hanging out with Jann Wenner, the editor/publisher of *Rolling Stone* magazine.

I knew about the work of Dr. Cohen, who began actively counseling against drug use after becoming a Meher Baba devotee. He seemed well placed to be a counselor, given his experience as one of the original "psychedelic guides" at Harvard University under Timothy Leary and Richard Alpert. I spoke to Delia about Cohen, and we thought it a good idea to bring his message on drugs and their effect on consciousness and the spiritual journey to Britain. He agreed to come over, and planning for the visit to London was in an advanced stage by the fall of '68. I had arranged a number of speaking engagements, including a talk organized by Jim Haynes at the London Arts Lab, and another at Beckenham Arts Lab, at the request of David Bowie.

During one of Dr. Cohen's visits to Britain, we arranged radio and TV interviews. One interview was for *The Timeless Moment: Experienced Through Drugs, Madness, and Mysticism*, a three-part series broadcast

the globe as metaphor
changing perspectives

The sixties provided a key moment of change when our perception of the Earth changed. As the human imagination mapped the birth of the universe and engineered a way out into the solar system, it reinforced the idea that we live in one global village on a planet with finite resources.

Over time, new technologies would devise better ways for global voices to communicate with each other while also creating the ability to annihilate each other at the touch of a button. Global trade and stock markets would come to overrule local issues and environmental concerns, and the scientific community would no longer consider ecological systems in stable equilibrium as the balance of nature became increasingly disturbed by human activity.

The development of satellite technology provided a platform for the first global television link-up with the broadcast of the BBC program *Our World* to a global audience. Popular culture was celebrated in the choice of The Beatles, singing "All You Need Is Love," for the British contribution to the festival of national cultures. The performance, broadcast live on June 25, 1967, from EMI Studios at Abbey Road, took place in a crowded Studio One among friends and figures from the London counterculture.

In the spring of 1968, Stanley Kubrick took the science-fiction genre and reimagined the story of space as an evolution of ideas outward from Earth to psychedelic self-consciousness in his film *2001: A Space Odyssey*. Sci-fi narratives had previously carried Cold War subtexts or, as in pulp fiction, imagined Earth under threat by alien invasions in stories of exotic alien worlds full of large-breasted women and creatures that looked like jellyfish. Kubrick described his film as "a journey from ape to angel"—a story of the origins and destiny of the human species. For me and my friends viewing the film's first screening in 1968, it encapsulated all that was profound and transcendental about the human race into space, which was viewed at that time as a collective experience for all.

In 1966, at Berkeley, California, the writer Stewart Brand questioned why we had not yet seen an image of the whole planet—an image that could promote the idea of Earth as one whole system, to be treated as a finite thing if we want to get civilization right. He believed one color image of the Earth—complete, tiny, and adrift—would do that. Two years later, NASA finally released just such an image: a picture of the whole Earth taken by astronaut Bill Anders during the Apollo 8 mission's lunar orbit on December 24, 1968. It is now considered to be the most influential environmental photograph ever taken. The photograph gave an image and title to Brand's new project, the *Whole Earth Catalog*. Considered the Google search engine of its day, its principal purpose was to share information that would improve newly formed alternative worlds. Brand realized that those developing communes across America's vast countryside needed tools, books, and ideas. His project created the first example of crowdsourcing after an appeal to send suggestions for items that communes would find helpful, with Brand offering to pay ten dollars for each item published. Contributors included Buckminster Fuller, with his designs for geodesic domes; the philosopher and media theorist Marshall McLuhan; and poet, writer, environmental activist, and farmer Wendell Berry.

The NASA photograph of Earth taken from the surface of the Moon corresponded with my thoughts on the *Tommy* cover. It is a profound existential image of a beautiful blue sphere in fragile balance with itself, hovering delicately in a seemingly infinite emptiness. I looked at that image when *Tommy* was released in May 1969, and it seemed an apt metaphor for the ideas I had considered when creating the cover.

An epic drama of adventure and exploration

Space Station One: your first step in an Odyssey that will take you to the Moon, the planets and the distant stars.

2001: a space odyssey

MGM PRESENTS A STANLEY KUBRICK PRODUCTION

CINERAMA Super Panavision® and Metrocolor

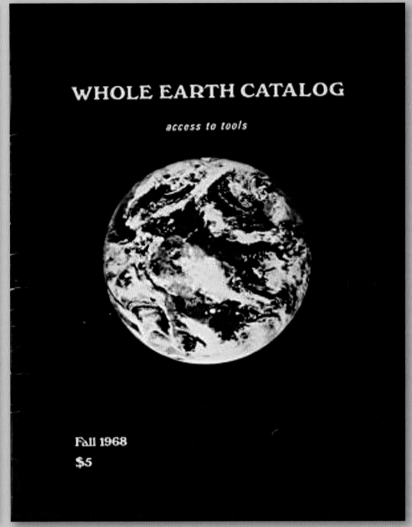

WHOLE EARTH CATALOG

access to tools

Fall 1968
$5

above left: A poster for Stanley Kubrick's *2001: A Space Odyssey*. "If anyone understands it on the first viewing," the director told *Playboy* interviewer Eric Norden in 1968, "we've failed in our intention."

above right: The first issue of *Whole Earth Catalog*, published by Stewart Brand in the fall of 1968, took its title from the first "whole Earth" image taken from space during the Apollo 8 lunar orbit.

❝ I intended the film to be an intensely subjective experience that reaches the viewer at an inner level of consciousness, just as music does . . . if *2001* succeeds at all, it is in reaching a wide spectrum of people who would not often give a thought to man's destiny, his role in the cosmos, and his relationship to higher forms of life."

Stanley Kubrick to *Playboy*, September 1968

"The Who turn up early and stop traffic, delivering a fiery version of 'A Quick One While He's Away,' their brief pre-*Tommy* foray into rock opera. Captured in top form (with Keith Moon still alive and well and slugging his drums), they are young, beautiful, and impervious in ways that give this film its accidental poignancy."

Janet Maslin on *The Rolling Stones Rock and Roll Circus*, *New York Times*, October 12, 1996

by the BBC and produced by Shirley Du Boulay. Part of filming for the episode on mysticism took place at Willoughby House and included interviews with Dr. Cohen, Pete, Katie, and myself; other contributors included the Reverend Ken Leech and Steve Abrams of the Society of Mental Awareness (SOMA). The interviews provided the opportunity to describe Meher Baba's anti-drug message and explain the benefits of mystic experience through spiritual means.

Prior to this, in September 1968, the BBC 2 TV channel broadcast *The Sound of Change*. Presented by cultural theorist Stuart Hall and sociologist Peter Worsley, it explored the history of popular music from skiffle to psychedelia, the nature of changing audiences, and the influence of the counterculture in the context of contemporary youth culture. The program included a performance by Pink Floyd and interviews with Pete Townshend, Mick Jagger, Allen Ginsberg, and Jim Haynes. Katie and I gave a brief account of our experience of the 14-Hour Technicolor Dream and a description of the event as a mass performance encouraging audience participation.

The Who rounded out the year with an appearance at the Rolling Stones' *Rock and Roll Circus*, taped in Wembley, London, on December 10–11. The Stones and a number of other acts, including John Lennon and Jethro Tull, were filmed on a makeshift circus stage. The results were due to be broadcast on television, but then the Stones pulled the plug, with some suggesting they did so because they felt they had been upstaged by The Who. "They weren't just usurped by The Who," Pete later told *Mojo* magazine. "They were also usurped by Taj Mahal—who was just, as always, extraordinary." (The footage was eventually released in 1996.)

A Phoenix Rising

Nineteen sixty-nine began with a shock. We were informed that Meher Baba had "dropped his body" on January 31. There had been plans to attend a mass *darshan* (public gathering) in Ahmednagar, Baba's hometown, but this was now in doubt following his passing. Things went ahead as planned, but Pete and I had already canceled our arrangements and were hitting a pressing *Tommy* deadline, so we did not go. The opportunity to meet Baba was now lost forever.

On July 20, 1969, the Apollo 11 *Eagle* module landed on the Moon, with Neil Armstrong stepping onto the surface in the Sea of Tranquility, closely followed by Buzz Aldrin. An image sent back to every TV screen on Earth showed a delicate, beautiful, bright blue circle hanging in an infinite black space, not unlike *Tommy*, a symbol of self both bound and limitless. For one brief moment, a worldwide audience would remember where they were on the planet and what they were doing, creating a shared memory of truly global proportions.

Tommy was a phoenix project—a giant leap for Pete and The Who. Its success would propel the group forward into the seventies on a trajectory as rock icons, elevating Roger from young mod to rock god and boosting Pete's musical ambitions ever further as he set to work first on the *Lifehouse* project (eventually realized as *Who's Next*) and then on *Quadrophenia*.

For me, it would provide new work horizons, with an agent in New York, awards at home, and an exhibition of my work at the Whitechapel Art Gallery in London. The new decade appeared full of possibilities.

2 the music

Chris Charlesworth

the music

In many ways, The Who's recording career up to *Tommy* can be seen as a template for their magnum opus. Indeed, a case can be made that the protagonist of their very first single as The Who was the prototype for the deaf, dumb, and blind boy.

The narrator of "I Can't Explain," recorded in November 1964, is **a frustrated teenager unable to express himself, not just to the girl of his dreams but also to the world at large, and although he's unencumbered by Tommy's sensory handicaps, there's more than a hint of the angst that Tommy Walker will endure.**

"I Can't Explain" appeared after The Beatles and Rolling Stones had emerged as the twin forerunners of the sixties beat boom. The Who—who in the fullness of time would occupy a sort of bronze-medal position behind them—were not just slow off the starting blocks but approached their calling from a different angle. The first ten singles released by The Beatles were love songs or songs that related in some way to relationships with the opposite sex, as were seven of the first eight released by the Stones. In contrast, it's hard to find a trace of romance in any of The Who's singles that followed "I Can't Explain." Pete Townshend's mind was thereafter focused on higher things: the generation gap, the plight of teenagers, communication or lack thereof, the futility of conformity, cross-dressing, sexual frustration, illusions and disillusionment. Much of this was seen through the prism of *mod*, the youth cult to which The Who had attached themselves during the brief period in 1964 when they were known as the High Numbers, and which clung to them throughout 1965 and '66.

Fortunately, Townshend had a knack of framing his rather lofty themes within a punchy three-minute pop song, so those for whom the lyrics went in one ear and out the other, or who simply didn't get what Roger Daltrey was singing about, could still appreciate the rush of a Who single, especially when Townshend's distorted guitar and Keith Moon's tireless drums played key roles.

More specifically, the musical seeds of *Tommy* can be traced back to The Who's second album, released in December 1966, side two of which is dominated by the closing track, "A Quick One" (also the album's title in Britain). Included largely because Daltrey and Moon had failed to come up with their quota of songs as per an agreement with the group's music publishers, "A Quick One" was in part Kit Lambert's solution for filling up the LP, but also a means to encourage Townshend to write an extended piece of music, thus fulfilling Kit's ambition to emulate in some way his illustrious composer father, Constant Lambert. Goaded by his manager, Townshend wrote a "mini-opera" that lasted just over nine minutes and sped through six connected sections, all with different melodies of their own, ranging from rather camp country and western to lush harmonies and all-out power-pop, with a touch of ribald English music hall in between. There was also a rousing power-chord climax, soon to become a distinctive Who trait, with quite stunning vocal harmonies that benefited from John Entwistle's ability to sing falsetto.

Once recorded, "A Quick One" soon became part of the group's stage act, debuted at London's Saville Theatre on January 29, 1967—a propitious occasion, with Jimi Hendrix also on the bill and John Lennon and Paul McCartney in the audience. "The Who were as wild and unpredictable as ever," wrote Chris Welch in the following week's *Melody Maker*, before going on to comment on the potential for rivalry between The Who and Hendrix. "It was a close battle . . . and fans will be arguing about the winners. Either way, two of Britain's most exciting groups thrilled the crowds with hard-hitting sights and sounds."

previous spread: The Who onstage at London's Saville Theatre, October 22, 1967. The Saville was leased by Beatles manager Brian Epstein from 1965 until his death in 1967, and Epstein presented both plays and rock concerts at the venue.

above: Townshend and Kit Lambert backstage at the Saville Theatre, October 22, 1967.

right: "I Can't Explain," The Who's first single under that name, was released January of 1965 in the United Kingdom and reached #8 in the British charts.

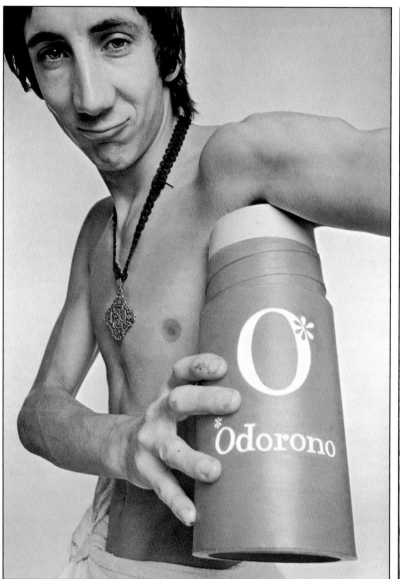

THE WHO SELL OUT

Replacing the stale smell of excess with
the sweet smell of success,
Peter Townshend, who, like nine out of ten stars,
needs it. Face the music with Odorono,
the all-day deodorant that
turns persperation into inspiration.

THE WHO SELL OUT

This way to a cowboy's breakfast.
Daltrey rides again. Thinks: "Thanks to Heinz
Baked Beans every day is a super day".
Those who know how many beans make five
get Heinz beans inside and outside at
every opportunity. Get saucy.

Crucially, playing "A Quick One" enabled The Who to come to terms with the complexities of performing a conjoined medley of several songs, albeit fairly short ones, moving from one to the next with effortless precision regardless of tempo changes or shifts in ambience. All of this would stand them in good stead when it came time to take their next, far longer and more ambitious rock opera on the road.

The Who's 1967 album, *The Who Sell Out*, contains precursors to *Tommy* that are even more unequivocal. There are hints of the opera's mood in "Odorono," a spoof deodorant commercial, and Entwistle's "Silas Stingy" seems like a blueprint for the "nasty" songs that Townshend requested he write for *Tommy*. Even more explicit is the coda to a lengthy and fairly enigmatic song called "Rael," which offers an early introduction to the melodic themes of "Sparks" and "Underture"—both key instrumental motifs of the opera.

An even bigger clue to what was going on in Townshend's mind, albeit hidden from public view at the time, was a song called "Glow Girl," which he wrote around this time, and which was recorded shortly after *Sell Out* was released. Though "Glow Girl" would not appear on record until 1974, on the outtakes LP *Odds and Sods* (and later as a bonus track on the 1995 reissue of *Sell Out*), it seems in hindsight to be the very first identifiable germ of *Tommy*. Ostensibly a song about a plane crash in which the protagonist sifts through the contents of her handbag as the aircraft descends, toward the end it includes the line, "It's a girl, Mrs Walker, it's a girl." With a gender change, these are among the opening lines to *Tommy*.

"['Glow Girl'] is rich in both melody and ideas and was to have influential repercussions," writes John Atkins in *The Who on Record*. "A great deal happens in a short duration . . . and the song encompasses Townshend's patent ringing guitar chords on the intro and an up-tempo verse pattern with a sure beat from Moon before a simulated plane crash effect gives way to a more placid coda in which the victim is reborn."

Tommy Walker, of course, would himself be reborn once he was cured of those annoying sensory impediments.

Amazing Journey

If by the time *Sell Out* was released *Tommy* wasn't yet a work in progress in the studio, it certainly was in Townshend's head. In 1967, he had moved into a flat on Ebury Street, in London's Belgravia. "I had nice big playback speakers and as usual when I was writing I would prepare demos before I even played them to the group or even suggested to the group that there might be the possibility of a song," he writes in *The Story of Tommy*. "The most fascinating thing about this studio was that it was the room in which the first few songs from *Tommy* were born."

Briefly lodging with Townshend and his girlfriend Karen Astley in Ebury Street at the time was Richard Stanley, a young filmmaker friend who recruited Townshend to appear in a twenty-four-minute avant-garde film called *Lone Ranger*. Townshend is seen driving his open-topped Lincoln Continental around the streets of central London, and also contributed guitar music to the soundtrack that bears more than a slight resemblance to the rhythmic foundation of *Tommy*. Back at the flat, he played the song "Welcome" to Stanley. "[The song] was about the value of friends," Townshend writes in his autobiography,

Who I Am. "When I played the demo to [Stanley] ... he thought I was using the song to invite him to partake in a ménage à trois."

The first public announcement by Townshend that he was working on a new and quite large-scale rock opera came in May 1968, when *Melody Maker*'s Chris Welch visited him at the flat and heard "Now I'm a Farmer," which Welch described as being "from the long-awaited Townshend opera which he has been working on, on and off, in different forms for a couple of years." "Farmer," of course, would not appear in *Tommy*, but Townshend told Welch, "I'm working on an opera which I did once before, and I am thinking of calling it *The Amazing Journey*. I've completed some of it and I'd like to put it out on an LP. The theme is about a deaf, dumb, and blind boy who has dreams and sees himself as a ruler of the cosmos."

On June 28, The Who opened an American tour that extended until August 30 and included a three-night stand at the Fillmore West in San Francisco. During the group's stay in the Bay Area, Townshend was interviewed at length by Jann Wenner, the editor and publisher of *Rolling Stone* magazine, and in a wide-ranging conversation outlined further ideas for *Tommy*. "We've been talking about doing an opera," he said. "What has basically happened is we've condensed all of these ideas, all of this energy and all these gimmicks and whatever we've decided upon for future albums, into one juicy package. The package I hope is going to be called *Deaf, Dumb, and Blind Boy*. It's a story about a kid that's born deaf, dumb, and blind, and what happened to him throughout his life."

Townshend then proceeded to take Wenner through the plot in some detail and at great length, mentioning the father's attitude toward his son's handicaps, a perverted uncle, what's happening inside Tommy's head, and many other elements. When published, the interview ran over eleven pages of two issues of Wenner's magazine. It also confirmed Townshend's position alongside Bob Dylan, John Lennon, Brian Wilson, and a handful of others as the leading lights among those musicians who were developing rock into an art form way above the disposable pop that in the past had done little more than to cause teenage girls to scream their heads off.

That US tour included a date at the Singer Bowl in New York, where The Who appeared with The Doors, the Los Angeles group fronted by provocative singer Jim Morrison. During The Doors' set, there were altercations between the audience and stagehands, and when a girl was manhandled and ended up with bad cuts to her face, Morrison callously declined from intervening. The incident became the inspiration for a Townshend song called "Sally Simpson."

Back in Britain, The Who began recording *Tommy* at IBC. Townshend had already demoed several songs, among them "Amazing Journey," an early draft for the opera that began life as a lengthy poem; "Sensation," about a girl he'd bedded on The Who's ill-fated Australian tour of early 1968; "Welcome," a peaceful, open-hearted, Meher Baba–inspired song; and "We're Not Gonna Take It," a protest against totalitarianism. Entwistle was assigned to write a couple of mildly offensive songs that Townshend felt were uncomfortably close to childhood experiences of his own: "Cousin Kevin," about Tommy's bullying cousin, and "Uncle Ernie," about a pedophile uncle who molests him.

right: The Who during a photo shoot in the Hollywood Hills, February 26, 1968.

getting the scoop
townshend's demos and home recordings

With the exception of The Beatles, groups who wrote and recorded their own material usually worked out songs among themselves at home before entering the studio, thus saving themselves hourly rates that could mount up and which were invariably charged back to the act by their record label.[2] The Who were different.

The group's songwriter, Pete Townshend, became fascinated with the working of recording studios very early on in his career, and soon built his own in which he could produce demos of his songs. These were then circulated to the members of the group to learn from, but during the sixties little was known about Townshend's secret solo recording habit. "For many years, recording was my one hobby," he writes in the liner notes to the first of his *Scoop* albums of demos. "It was only the people close to me who heard the music I made for myself or by myself. I have always called these recordings 'demos' . . . whether they were made for my own amusement, for film soundtracks, for experimental purposes, or to submit material for The Who."

The earliest indicator that Pete Townshend's recording activities were not confined to sessions with The Who occurred in 1970, on an album called *Happy Birthday*, a limited-edition tribute album to Meher Baba to which he contributed, among other tracks, a demo of "The Seeker," which The Who would release as a single that same year. What was interesting about it was that Townshend played everything—guitar, bass, piano, and drums—and double-tracked his voice over the top. Less expressive than The Who's version, and taken at a slower tempo, it nevertheless shed light on Townshend's method as a writer, and on how he communicated his songs to the three other members of The Who.

Happy Birthday was soon bootlegged, as was a subsequent Meher Baba tribute album called *I Am*, which contains a lengthy instrumental version of "Baba O'Riley," all of which prompted MCA Records in America to propose that to thwart the bootleggers Townshend make a commercially available solo album. *Who Came First*, which contains more solo tracks, was released in 1972, with proceeds going to the Baba Foundation. By now, the cat was out of the bag. Townshend had made scores of private recordings in his home studio, some for use by The Who as guide demos, some for others, and some for his own personal use.

The triple-LP *Glastonbury Fayre*, released in 1972, includes a beautiful Townshend ballad called "Classified," which would not otherwise become available until it appeared as the B-side to his 1980 single "Let My Love Open the Door," again only as a demo. Also included on the B-side was Pete's demo of "Greyhound Girl," written for the *Lifehouse* project. Who fans who bought a copy of Richard Barnes's 1982 book *The Who: Maximum R&B* were offered an unexpected treat: a flexi-disc single within its pages of "My Generation" and "Pinball Wizard," recorded as demos by Townshend, with him singing and playing all the instruments. Then, in 1983, came *Scoop*, a double LP of his demos, followed in 1987 by *Another Scoop*, and in 2001 by *Scoop 3*. In all, eighty-six Townshend demos have been made available in these collections.

On the inner sleeve of the first *Scoop* album, Townshend provided details of all his home studios, from his parents' house in Ealing (Studio One), where he made tapes in 1964, through to his house by the Thames in Twickenham (Studio Six), where he built a control room and studio in two adjacent rooms that were crammed with recording equipment. Along the way he passed through Belgravia (Studio Two), Chelsea (Three), Wardour Street (Four), and Ebury Street (Five), also in Belgravia, where *Tommy* was born. In 1976, Townshend bought Oceanic Studios, by the Thames between Richmond and

right: Townshend in his home studio at 87 Wardour Street in the heart of London's Soho, late 1966.

left and opposite: Townshend at work at his home studio in Twickenham, 1970. His Thames-side home was a stone's throw away from Eel Pie Island, where The Who played on October 30, 1968.

Twickenham, and renamed it Eel Pie Studios. Originally a boathouse, its location enabled Townshend to get there by boat from his house on the other side of the river. It became a commercial studio until Townshend sold it in 2008, and thereafter it became a private residence.

It could be argued that "Sunrise" on *A Quick One* in 1966 was a solo recording, since none of The Who bar Townshend appeared on the track, and the same applies to "Tommy's Holiday Camp" from *Tommy*. Of the songs that he demoed for *Tommy*, only "Pinball Wizard" and "Christmas" have appeared on the *Scoop* series. The remainder were made available on one of the four discs within the Super Deluxe Edition of *Tommy* that was released in 2013, which also includes four tracks that did not appear in the opera. The first, "Dream One," is an elongated prelude to "Sparks," which, when it arrives, is over seven minutes long—as opposed to two minutes on the *Tommy* LP—and thus seems like the foundation of "Underture,"

while the second is a ten-second piece entitled "Success" that sounds as if it was written for the moment when Tommy's mum and dad realize their son can hear, speak, and see. The third, credited to The Who (though there's no trace of Daltrey), is a stodgily repetitive, riff-based song called "Trying to Get Through." Whoever made the decision to omit it from the opera made a good call.

The final track is a top-quality studio recording of "Young Man Blues" by The Who, and its inclusion on this CD of demos confirms it was recorded during the *Tommy* sessions. This was originally intended as a stopgap single while they were recording *Tommy*, but in the event was included on *The House That Track Built*, a 1969 UK-only sampler from The Who's label, Track Records. A slower alternate studio take became a bonus track on the extended *Odds and Sods* CD in 1998, but neither compares favorably to the many live versions available.

Expectations that the album would be finalized before Christmas, so as to appear in the shops for the holiday season, were soon dashed, not least because the group needed to keep working on the live circuit to put bread on the table. Indeed, between the start of the *Tommy* sessions in September and their conclusion around the following March, The Who played something like fifty concerts in Britain, including an intensive two-shows-a-night UK tour between November 8 and 20, with their friends the Small Faces also on the bill at most shows.

"Myths have grown up around the recording of *Tommy*," writes Townshend in *Who I Am*. "One is that we spent a lot of time in the studio discussing my ideas, trying to help me solve problems. This happened occasionally but not often. Roger remembers it this way, but perhaps that's because as a singer he was often waiting for long periods for us to complete tracks on which he could sing. Keith said we all pulled together as a group to make *Tommy* happen. As a band that's true but there were plenty of times when I tried to explain the more personal shades of the *Tommy* story to my mates, and they simply weren't interested."

The views of the other members of The Who sketch a rather different picture to the one painted by Townshend. "Pete used to come in some days with just half a demo," said Daltrey, effectively contradicting the guitarist. "We used to talk for hours, literally. We probably did as much talking as we did recording. We spent weeks sorting out arrangements for the music."

"He was writing songs and putting them together like a jigsaw," said Moon. "When we went into the studio it was still in bits and pieces. Pete would say, 'Well, what do you think of this bit?' and then John or someone would come up with an idea and then gradually it became a group effort."

Entwistle went even further in expressing the collective bewilderment that settled around the group during the recording sessions. "All I knew is that when we were recording the damn thing nobody knew what it was all about or how it would end," he said. "It was only when it was decided to make *Tommy* into a double album instead of a single that it became much easier to work out a story line."

If there were occasions when the other three came to doubt Townshend's sanity, then in the final reckoning he was touchingly appreciative of their patience. "I mean, what other three musicians would have put up with my bullshit in order to get this album out," he mused. "It's my apple. It's my whole Baba trip. And they just sat there, let it all come out, and then leapt upon it and gave it an extra boot. It's an incredible group to write for, because you know it's going to work out right."

Making Overtures

Kit Lambert, The Who's co-manager, certainly played a key role in the proceedings. While his partner, Chris Stamp, concerned himself with the nuts and bolts of group management—booking dates, promotion, money issues—Lambert became a creative foil for Townshend. Most managers of groups left their charges to get on with the artistic side of things, but Lambert's background in and knowledge of "serious" music gave him an understanding of classical

" We're working quite hard at the moment
—we spend every day recording numbers for our
new album. It's like going to the office every day
—we've set aside the hours between two in the
afternoon and midnight for recording, and we
try to stick to it."

John Entwistle to *Melody Maker*, November 9, 1968

above: Kit Lambert with Entwistle, Daltrey, and
Townshend at IBC Studios during the recording of
Tommy, October 1968.

opposite left: "A camp with a difference, never mind
the weather"—British holidaymakers enjoy the charms
of the Butlin's holiday camp in Pwllheli, Wales, May 1961.

opposite right: The American jazz and blues musician
Mose Allison, a cover version of whose "Eyesight to the
Blind" featured on *Tommy*.

opera that was probably unique in the rock world, enabling him to give important pointers to the untutored Townshend. As well as boosting Townshend's confidence, his advice impacted significantly on the development of the opera.

Nevertheless, the extent of Lambert's role in the creation of *Tommy* will forever be shrouded in uncertainty. Townshend has denied that Lambert "completed and guided the story around *Tommy*," as some have suggested, though he concedes that Lambert made valuable contributions, including suggesting The Who record an overture to the piece. He also spent some time typing out a plotline for everyone's benefit—a document that suggests Lambert may have had a hidden agenda that leaned toward turning *Tommy* into a screenplay for a movie at some future date.

In the section devoted to Kit in his book on three male generations of the Lambert family, the writer Andrew Motion showers credit on Kit, stating, "Short of writing the songs themselves, Kit could not have done more to give *Tommy* its final shape," but then concedes that while Kit kept The Who's motor ticking over, his suggestions were not always acted upon. A key issue was whether or not The Who should record *Tommy* with a symphony orchestra—a proposal of Lambert's that Townshend decisively countermanded each time the subject was mentioned. Townshend believed strongly that because it was his concept, the group should play every instrument themselves.

Similarly, Motion reproaches Lambert for the flat production—a fault that prompted Entwistle to compare the sound of the drums to "biscuit tins," which was a bit of an exaggeration in light of

Moon's generous contribution to *Tommy*—but the sound of the original vinyl record *was* generally muddy, a fault that more than likely could be attributed to the technical imperfections of the equipment at IBC.

"The blame for this must lie with Kit," writes Motion. "He was more interested in capturing what [Richard] Barnes called 'the musical essence' than in producing the best possible technical quality."

As regards the plot, Daltrey, Entwistle, and Moon had every reason to be confused, not least because when the sessions for the opera began, Townshend had by no means completed the song cycle. At some point he decided to include a version of Sonny Boy Williamson's 1951 blues "Born Blind," which eight years later had been re-recorded in a swing-jazz arrangement as "Eyesight to the Blind" by Mose Allison, a white American jazz pianist whose work Townshend admired. One idea that certainly did come from a group discussion was Moon's proposal, probably made as a joke, that Tommy might become the host at a Butlins-style holiday camp—a suggestion that Townshend rather liked, so he wrote a burlesque-styled "throwaway fragment" in which Uncle Ernie, Moon's partner in spirit, welcomes Tommy's disciples to his holiday camp.

Far more crucial to the success of the project, however, was the writer Nik Cohn's idea that Tommy might become a pinball champion—a suggestion that came late in the proceedings but in many ways gave Tommy an identity that is now widely recognized as the unfortunate boy's defining attribute.

the man behind the curtain
introducing kit lambert

Of all the schemers and dreamers, duckers and divers drawn to the pop industry in the wake of The Beatles, the maddest, baddest, and most dangerous to know was Kit Lambert.

Christopher Sebastian Lambert was born on May 11, 1935, in Knightsbridge, London; public school and Oxford educated, posh-speaking, cultured in the arts, multilingual, sophisticated epicurean, former army officer and jungle explorer, unrepentant gay libertine, willfully disregardful of conventional behavior and virtues, and the most financially irresponsible rock entrepreneur ever to sign a contract.

Family genes contributed to his extraordinary character. His Russian grandfather, George, became Australia's foremost war artist, while his father, Constant, was a classical composer and acclaimed music critic. Constant and his model wife, Florence, split up when Kit was two, and thereafter their son, an only child, was educated at Lancing College near Brighton and at Oxford, where he spent much of his time drinking while experimenting with his conflicted sexuality. National Service, most of it spent in Hong Kong, was followed by an expedition to trace the source of the River Iriri in Brazil, on which a close friend was hacked to death—and scalped—by a tribe of Indians. Lambert—scared out of his wits, ravaged by tropical insects, and dangerously ill—somehow managed to survive.

On his return, he opted for a career in film, which led to a friendship with skirt-chasing Chris Stamp, brother of the actor Terence, whose background as the son of an East End tugboat skipper was far removed from Kit's upper-class Bohemian upbringing. That he and Stamp should engage with The Who—themselves a combination of extreme personalities on a par with their own—seems in hindsight to be one of the most perfect acts of symbiosis in the history of pop. At the time, though, it precipitated chaos of the grandest order, out of which emerged an alliance that forever altered the course of popular music.

"As solemn management, it's always been farcical," writes Nik Cohn in *Awopbopaloobopalopbamboom*, his seminal primer of pop. "Almost everyone involved is a maniac, almost everyone is extremely bright and hardly a week goes by without some kind of major trauma." That Lambert and Stamp knew absolutely nothing about the music business probably acted in their favor, since everything they did broke all previous rules.

Brimming with ideas born of his headstrong genius, Lambert's influence on The Who was incalculable. He encouraged their violent stage act and ear-splitting volume; he introduced the concept of stage lighting and making short promotional films ("videos," in today's parlance); and he encouraged them to behave as if they were far more successful than they actually were, thus hastening their descent into chronic debt. Perhaps most importantly, he encouraged Pete Townshend's songwriting ambitions by buying him two Vortexion tape recorders, in the process ensuring the guitarist's eternal loyalty.

In 1964, Lambert signed a production deal with expatriate US producer Shel Talmy . . . then broke it in circumstances that proved financially catastrophic. As a result, Lambert became The Who's record producer himself, and, in time, a very good one. He begged, stole, and borrowed to stay solvent, while at the same time he and Stamp creamed off 40 percent of The Who's earnings between them. When it became clear to them that record companies made far more money than artists, the pair formed their own label,

> **"** Kit taught Keith about wine, about fancy restaurants. But Keith turned Kit on to pills. They always had an incredible strange affinity."
>
> Chris Stamp to Tony Fletcher, *Dear Boy*

above: Lambert, Townshend, and Daltrey during the recording of "The Seeker" at IBC Studios, London, January 19, 1970.

Track Records, signing Jimi Hendrix, among others. Track was among the first independent rock labels in the UK—a blueprint for dozens that would follow—and an immense cash cow.

While Stamp busied himself promoting The Who in America, Lambert produced all of The Who's post-1965 hit singles and albums, including *A Quick One* (which, at Kit's suggestion, included Townshend's first extended work), *The Who Sell Out*, and *Tommy*. As the creative foil for Townshend, Lambert was a key element in *Tommy*, mapping out an early rough narrative for the project and encouraging its composer all the way. Kit reveled in its success and took pride in presenting The Who at opera houses in Europe and America.

"He educated me by encouraging me," Townshend told Lambert biographer and former British Poet Laureate Andrew Motion. "It's what made him a great mentor. He could see that I was at my best when I was dealing with my conscience."

"Kit's greatest contribution to The Who . . . was his unrelenting expansion and projection of Townshend's fantasies and ideas," writes Who biographer Dave Marsh. He was also a man for the grand gesture. "Kit often used to fantasize about doing things on a grand scale," Townshend told Marsh. "It was him pushing us to do things in a grander way . . . [he] was telling me I was a great writer. And I believed him because I wanted to believe him."

Lambert influenced the group in other, less professional, ways too. "[He] was largely responsible for setting the example of preposterously high standards of living Keith demanded for himself throughout his life," writes Tony Fletcher in *Dear Boy*, his Moon biography.

"Kit thought that he would sophisticate these working-class boys," Who associate Richard Barnes told Fletcher. "He would introduce them to the world of restaurants and other things that in those days you didn't go to. He only tried it with Pete and Keith. Pete was obviously intelligent, at art school, looking for the deeper meaning, and Moon was just way alive and full of energy."

Whatever closeness Lambert enjoyed socially with The Who—Townshend and Moon in particular—*Tommy* proved to be his last gasp with the group. In 1971, after a series of disastrous, drug- and alcohol-fueled recording sessions in New York, the band opted to use Glyn Johns as their producer for what became *Who's Next*, and the relationship never recovered. By this time, Kit's recklessness had extended toward The Who's financial affairs, prompting Roger Daltrey to demand his resignation. "We'd been screwed up the fucking alley," said the singer. A reluctant Townshend had to agree. After a struggle, Lambert and Stamp gave up control of the group in 1975, handing over the reins to their subordinate, the far more prudent Bill Curbishley, who looks after the band's affairs to this day.

By this time, Kit was dividing his time between increasingly squalid West London flats and a Venetian palace he'd bought with his share of the *Tommy* royalties. With creditors baying at his heels, in 1976 he was made a ward of court to prevent them forcing bankruptcy proceedings—a procedure that resulted in Lambert receiving a small weekly stipend on which to live. It was never enough.

There followed five years of idle misery, exacerbated by alcoholism and a decade-long addiction to heroin. Kit's last encounter with The Who was in Frejus, France, in May 1979, during the group's first shows

with Kenney Jones on drums in place of the departed Moon. "The band seemed very happy to see him," says Who sleeve designer Richard Evans, who was backstage that night. "He had a touch of the Brian Wilsons about him, sort of not all there . . . a bit scruffy, too, but he was always that way."

Townshend, too, was upbeat about the encounter. "Kit Lambert has just spent fifteen minutes telling me what's wrong with The Who—and he was right," he told reporters afterward.

But there was to be no rebirth for Kit. By the time of this sighting, he had squandered everything and was living back in London, either dossing down at the homes of long-suffering friends or staying at

his mother's house in Fulham. He would die in April 1981, virtually destitute, in an Acton hospital from a brain hemorrhage incurred after falling down her staircase. The previous night he'd been beaten up in the toilets of a gay nightclub in Earls Court, allegedly over a drug debt. At least one mourner at his cremation ducked as the coffin slid into the furnace, convinced that it would explode with all the alcohol and chemicals inside him.

In a wonderful piece of understatement, Andrew Motion wrote of Kit, "His impetuosity and his relish for living at risk seemed not to include any fully developed appreciation of the difficulties into which he might be led."

> " Pete was cunning: he slipped in a song called 'Pinball Wizard' so that I would be seduced to write a rave article for the *New York Times*. Of course, I fell for it head-on and immediately leapt into print . . . announcing that *Tommy* was the greatest thing since *Cosi fan tutte* and 'I'm Forever Blowing Bubbles.'"

Nik Cohn to *Radio Times*, October 5–11, 1974

A pal of both Lambert and Townshend, Cohn was an innovative and occasionally abrasive rock critic, then working for *The Observer* in London while also penning reviews for the *New York Times*. Seeking to get Cohn on side so as to assure a positive review when the album was finally released, Lambert invited him to listen to work on *Tommy* thus far. "Nik was appalled at the idea of a rock opera," Townshend writes in the sheet music book *The Decade of the Who*. "He felt it sounded pompous and The Who were losing their street feel. As he was a pinball addict I wrote this song, ensuring his enthusiasm."

Agreeing that *Tommy* needed something a bit lighter to balance his spiritual message, Townshend rushed home and wrote "Pinball Wizard." In subsequent interviews, Townshend admitted to feeling that the song was derisory, something "knocked off" quickly without much thought put into it. However, the other members of the group thought differently when they heard his demo. Bemused by their reaction, he would add that the only reason he wrote "Pinball Wizard" in the first place was to secure a positive review from Cohn, whom he knew to be a pinball fanatic.

"These two late additions to the plot [holiday camps and pinball], were pivotal in preventing the story from being drowned in spiritual piety," writes Tony Fletcher in *Dear Boy*, his definitive biography of Keith Moon. "Indeed, their familiar human themes remained in the listeners' minds long after Meher Baba's influence was forgotten."

With pinball and holiday camp references inserted into other songs, the album sessions stretched into 1969, by which time it had become clear that *Tommy* would become a double LP. This allowed more space for the "Overture," soon to become a rousing initiation to all that would follow; a few brief vocal intrusions that hurried the plot along and went some way to clarifying what was going on; and a thrilling ten-minute "Underture" instrumental, in which this particular theme is explored in every way possible.

Although Kit Lambert is credited as the producer of *Tommy*—and Damon Lyon-Shaw as engineer—there is plenty of evidence to suggest that Townshend himself deserves a production credit alongside them. Lambert's role, after all, was principally in cheerleading and holding the project together, like the producer of a film, while Lyon-Shaw's was sound balance in the control room. Perhaps "auteur" is a better description of Townshend's role. Not only was he becoming increasingly proficient in the studio—he claims his first production was "Substitute," as good a single as The Who ever recorded, in 1966—but during the *Tommy* sessions he took time out to produce "Something in the Air" by Thunderclap Newman, a group assembled around pianist Andy Newman, whom Townshend had met while at art school. A magnificent song and production, it reached #1 in the UK charts in July 1969—ironically, a feat The Who would never achieve.

The last-booked *Tommy* session was on March 7, whereupon Kit Lambert flew off to Cairo for a holiday, leaving the mixing to Lyon-Shaw and assistant engineer Ted Sharp. This was completed in April, for release in May. Meanwhile, The Who played a handful of gigs and settled down to intensive rehearsals. In the midst of it all—on March 28—Pete Townshend's wife Karen gave birth to their first daughter.

above left: "Sure plays a mean pinball." The decision to make Tommy a "Pinball Wizard" was largely down to Townshend's friendship with writer Nik Cohn, who was a pinball fanatic.

above right: Thunderclap Newman—*left to right:* John "Speedy" Keen, Jimmy McCulloch, and Andy Newman—whose "Something in the Air," produced by Townshend, was #1 in the UK singles chart for three weeks in July 1969. Keen doubled as Townshend's chauffeur.

“ The album concept in general is complex . . . we've been talking about a whole lot of things, and what has basically happened is that we've condensed all of these ideas, all this energy, and all these gimmicks, and whatever we've decided on for future albums, into one juicy package.”

Pete Townshend to *Rolling Stone*, September 28, 1968

above: Townshend listens to a *Tommy* playback at IBC Studios, October 1968. Townshend was born into a musical family: his father, Cliff, was a professional saxophone player, and his mother, Betty, a singer.

> It was quite a heavy story told in quite a heavy way. The way it worked out actually was like literature. It wasn't meant to happen that way, but nothing happened in *Tommy* itself that wasn't meant to happen."

Pete Townshend to *Melody Maker*, July 19, 1969

Deaf, Dumb, and Blind

In a nutshell, the story of *Tommy* is about how the infant Tommy Walker is rendered deaf, dumb, and blind through witnessing, in a mirror, the murder of his mother's lover by his father.[3] Having impregnated his wife before he went off to fight in World War II, and now believed dead, Tommy's father's return is as unexpected as it is evidently traumatic. Bullied and abused, he thereafter exists in an impenetrable shell while his parents seek a cure for his disabilities, among them exposure to a gypsy who prescribes psychedelic drugs. He comes to life only when confronted by pinball machines, on which he displays remarkable proficiency due to his inflated sense of touch. Miraculously cured when a mirror into which he is gazing is abruptly smashed, Tommy ascends to a position of celebrity as a Messiah-like figure who preaches spiritual enlightenment to his many followers.

This story is told by The Who in song over four vinyl sides of, for them, largely restrained rock music—almost ninety minutes' worth —in which the form is explored every which way with extraordinary precision and timing. The record as a whole is a primer on rock riffs, interlocking rhythms, electric and acoustic guitar backing, fluid bass lines, top flight drumming, singing, vocal harmonies, and every other skill with which a premier league rock band ought to be equipped. There is an almost mathematical precision to *Tommy* in the way that its musical motifs—the sharp "Go to the Mirror" riff, the shimmering "Pinball" intro, the dramatic "See Me, Feel Me" chorus, the undulating "Underture" / "Sparks" dynamics—are introduced in the overture, then repeated at various moments throughout. Because these motifs crop up repeatedly in this manner, *Tommy* becomes much easier to

assimilate on first listening than a double album of twenty or more non-interconnected songs.

Onstage, *Tommy* took on a whole other dimension—that's where it *really* became great, an issue we'll explore in the Legacy chapter that follows—but it's The Who's recorded version that is the essence and cornerstone of the whole *Tommy* mythos. The original album, opulently packaged in a beautifully designed, surreal, triple-gatefold sleeve complete with libretto, was—by current standards—poorly produced and/or mixed in the studio, and sounds very flat compared to certain other records in The Who's catalogue. This can be attributed to an administrative issue at IBC where, as Damon Lyon-Shaw has since explained, the mixing wasn't done in the main Studio A—where *Tommy* was recorded, and which he would have preferred—but in Studio B, where the desk was inferior.

The subsequent single-CD version from 1996, on which every song was remixed by Jon Astley and Andy Macpherson and remastered by Bob Ludwig, is a vast improvement. Further double-CD versions, produced by Pete Townshend, are better still and include outtakes and demos, and a live version largely recorded in Ottawa in 1969.[4] The 2001 reissue of The Who's *Live at Leeds* album on two CDs also includes a live version, as does the double-CD edition of their performance at 1970's Isle of Wight Festival. The definitive studio version to own is the Super Audio CD hybrid edition released in 2004. Remastered in proper studio 5.1 surround stereo, *Tommy* becomes a sonic *tour de force* that has to be heard to be believed. (A listing of all the significant versions of *Tommy* to have been released appears elsewhere in this book.)

It's a Boy

Like classical operas by Mozart, Verdi, and Tchaikovsky, *Tommy* opens with its "Overture." Eight portentously descending chords, beginning at C major, are played on guitar, bass, piano, and drums and repeated while an acoustic guitar strums beneath them—a striking introduction to a theatrically arranged segue of instrumental interpretations of the songs that will follow, most of them fairly brief and linked together by the rumbling, bass-heavy riff that will later accompany Tommy's relationship with mirrors. The guitar parts are played mainly on Townshend's acoustic Gibson J-200, which establishes a buoyant mood for the entire work, a shade or two mellower than might be expected from the group that recorded "My Generation." Entwistle's French horn takes on a melodic role in place of absent vocals, including a sort of fanfare at the beginning, while the choral chanting and drums are impressively symphonic. Indeed, in many respects, Keith Moon's work on *Tommy* represents his greatest contribution to The Who's entire catalogue. Now at his peak as a percussionist, he grabbed the opportunity to become an entire orchestra within himself, most notably on the lengthy and occasionally breathtaking instrumental track "Underture." Nevertheless, the best moment in the overture comes toward the end, when a Hammond B-3 organ arrives to pound out the "Listening to You" melody, at which point the arrangement moves up a notch or three, followed by the first glimpse of the soon-to-be-sanctified "Pinball" strum.

At the close of the overture, Townshend is left strumming alone for a segue into "It's a Boy," a brief introductory piece about Tommy's birth, sung by the guitarist in a high register; followed by some impressive acoustic guitar work that leads into "1921," a plaintive, melodic song, again sung by Townshend alone, the first of several delightful ballads he wrote for *Tommy*. This is intercut with a harsher refrain in which Tommy's parents urge their young son to forget the murder he's just witnessed from the reflection in the mirror—with disastrous consequences. Without this section and with perhaps an extra verse, "1921" was sufficiently mellifluous to have become a hit in its own right, perhaps sung by a girl. (In the United States, "1921" was titled "You Didn't Hear It.")

It is followed by "Amazing Journey," Daltrey's entry into the fray, and it is immediately clear that The Who's specialist singer has been practicing his scales—or has perhaps taken the group's anti-smoking song "Little Billy" to heart and cut down on his cigarette habit. The first truly great rock song on the album, "Amazing Journey" is a cornerstone for the whole *Tommy* project, contrasting Moon's "lead-the-way" drums with the lighter timbre that Daltrey would adopt for most of what he was required to sing in the role of *Tommy*. One of the many *Tommy* songs that came to life onstage, "Amazing Journey" segues into the deep-rooted, rumbling, endlessly repeated prelude to "Sparks," a juxtaposition intended to emphasize the confusion within Tommy's unbalanced mind. It then runs smoothly into the dynamics of "Sparks" itself, the instrumental refrain first heard in "Rael" on *The Who Sell Out*, which, as we shall see, is explored in far greater depth during "Underture." Onstage, "Sparks" became a *pièce de résistance* of ensemble Who playing, with the band reaching higher and higher toward those block-chord climaxes that defined their style. Here, they adopt a far lighter approach.

"Eyesight to the Blind" by Sonny Boy Williamson, the only non-Who song on *Tommy*, is a brief excursion—referred to as "The Hawker" in the libretto—into a bluesy form. The sharpest, most strident number thus far, with Moon answering Townshend's staccato guitar with rolls around the toms, it includes several references to Tommy's handicaps, thus helping to further the plot and in this context sounds for all the world as if it was written specifically for *Tommy*.[5]

"Christmas," with its nagging, slightly off-key, wavering background vocals by Entwistle and Townshend, is upbeat and vaguely unnerving, and seems designed to establish Tommy Walker's isolation from other children. He doesn't understand the meaning of Christmas—or anything very much. At its heart is an early preview of the "See Me, Feel Me" motif, sung sensitively by Daltrey in a call-and-response sequence with Townshend's more clamorous "Tommy can you hear me?" lines.

Entwistle's first *Tommy* song, "Cousin Kevin," befits the offbeat, often tongue-in-cheek, macabre style of many other songs the bass player wrote for The Who that characterized him as a rather ghoulish character, typified by the spider pendent he invariably wore on a chain around his neck. Tommy's encounter with his evil cousin Kevin, the school bully, is far from pleasant; he endures a ducking in the bath, cigarette burns, and being pushed down the stairs, among other unspeakable cruelties. A rather slight song, the vocal is pitched quite high—supposedly a deliberate ploy on Entwistle's part to ensure that he, and not Daltrey, would get to sing it onstage.

"Cousin Kevin" is followed by another *Tommy* highlight, "The Acid Queen," featuring Townshend on vocals for what appears to be an overtly drug-oriented song with a strong rock tempo and an infectious hook, but there's more to it than meets the eye. Townshend would later note, "The song's not just about acid; it's the whole drug thing, the drink thing, the sex thing wrapped into one big ball. It's about how you get it laid on you that if you haven't fucked forty birds, taken sixty trips, drunk fourteen pints or whatever . . . society—people—force it on you. She represents this force."

For many, "Underture," which follows, is the highpoint of the whole album. Effectively an elongated version of the coda from "Rael" on *The Who Sell Out*—or "Sparks"—played on guitar in its entirety, it is Keith Moon's crowning glory; his best ever work on record. Here we have The Who presented as an orchestra, the nearest thing to a (mini) symphony they ever recorded, just over ten minutes of spellbinding, ethereal enchantment; the perfect fusion of electric and acoustic guitar, bass, and drums, with a wash of wordless choral flight here and there to add to the intensity. The melody is simple enough, the cyclical leitmotifs first introduced in "Rael" here given a lighter, more delicate, touch; John's descending bass figure the rigid staff around which Pete and Keith can dance, increasingly willfully, as "Underture" takes root and grows. Having laid down the basic parts on his Gibson jumbo acoustic, Pete turned to electric for the lead parts, never overstating the riffs or playing with excess volume or treble tone; the simplicity of the piece is thus maintained, quite gorgeously, as it returns again and again to its source, the ringing open notes, the octave drops, and wave after wave of escalating crescendos.

left: Townshend gives the cameraman
the eye during the *Tommy* sessions at
IBC Studios, October 1968.

right: Entwistle and Townshend recording *Tommy*, IBC Studios, October 1968. Having played together since their teens, the pair had built up an intuitive musical relationship wherein Entwistle could predict what Townshend was about to play, thus enabling The Who to fly off at unexpected tangents onstage, then return on cue to the root of a song.

But, really, "Underture" belongs to Keith Moon. We'll never know how long it took him to record his parts, his cymbal washes, kettledrum rumbles, and skittering snare parts. I like to think he did it quickly, intuitively, for he was never a man to dawdle in anything he did. Tony Fletcher put it best in *Dear Boy*. "Moon gives up his rigidity and throws himself with great delight into the emotion of the music . . . matching Townshend's guitar rhythms beat for syncopated beat before ducking and diving around the back of the other instruments: he knows exactly when to fill the gaps with imaginative flourishes, and he knows exactly when to leave the spaces wide open too. . . . All in all, 'Underture' is the number that most clearly removes itself from the pantheon of music that had preceded *Tommy*. It's too raw to be classical, though Moon and Townshend's sense of dynamics would do any orchestral conductor proud; it's too well-structured in conventional chord patterns to be jazz; but it's way beyond whatever had passed for pop or rock in the past."

Pinball Wizardry

Moon's kettledrums bring "Underture" and the first vinyl disc to a suitably imposing close. The second opens with "Do You Think It's Alright," a quick vocal link into Entwistle's second song, "Fiddle About," which tells of further dreadful experiences that Tommy endures, this time at the hands of the family pervert. The wicked Uncle Ernie, presumably Kevin's dad, would eventually become synonymous with Moon's more depraved caricatures. Here, it's a mildly amusing comic piece, a hint of music hall, which, like "Cousin Kevin," sounds a bit out of place amid the profundity of Townshend's songs.

Thankfully, it is followed by "Pinball Wizard," another contender for the record's finest moment. Townshend has often been acclaimed as the greatest rhythm guitarist in rock, and no better evidence survives than the furious acoustic strumming that underpins this, the best-known song from *Tommy* and a song that in the fullness of time became a mandatory rite of passage at every Who concert thereafter. Recorded toward the end of the *Tommy* sessions, "Pinball" is a rock *tour de force*, brimful of ideas, power chords, great lyrics, and tight ensemble playing from the opening chord descent to the upward key change near the end. The concept of a deaf, dumb, and blind pinball champion might stretch the imagination, but anything can be forgiven in the context of this song.

It is difficult now to imagine *Tommy* without "Pinball," Townshend strumming that inimitable intro, playing the guitar like he was ringing a bell, punctuated by the thunderous sound of the powerful guitar stabs that Entwistle reproduced live by hammering down on his bottom bass string. That its composer considered it an insignificant knockoff immediately after he'd written it seems incomprehensible in the light of the status it now commands in The Who's repertoire. Its success caused Townshend to revise these opinions completely, not just in terms of its musical heft but as a key component of *Tommy*. "What it did," he said in 2016, "was inject this silly, colorful, daft notion into the whole thing, which in actual fact totally redeemed [Tommy] and also created a much better focus for my notion that somebody who was deaf, dumb, and blind could do something miraculous."

"There's a Doctor" is a quick link into "Go to the Mirror," a key song insofar as this is the point at which Tommy discovers he can see his

see me, feel me
the who at woodstock

It is Sunday, August 17, 1969, the dead of night, and The Who are about to perform in front of one of the biggest audiences of their career at the Woodstock Music and Arts Fair at Bethel, just over one hundred miles north of New York City.

Most estimates suggest that as many as four hundred thousand are in attendance, but disorganization means the band's appearance occurs eight hours later than planned, and, in the meantime, they have inadvertently sipped drinks laced with LSD. The delay, the acid, and the difficulty their tour manager has experienced in extracting the balance of the group's $12,500 fee from the promoters means they are all in a foul temper. Finally, at around 4 a.m., they take the stage.

The guitarist, who two years earlier had sworn off psychedelic drugs, is in the foulest mood of all. Skinny, sullen, and truculent, he stands on the right and is dressed in pristine white overalls—a "onesie" in today's parlance—the garb a house painter might wear for work, loose fitting so as to conceal the knee pads he wears to cushion his limbs against hard landings. He plays a dark red Gibson SG guitar very aggressively, treating it with contempt, occasionally spinning his right arm around like a Catherine wheel, leaping around the stage like a gymnast crossed with a ballet dancer, forever on the move. In complete contrast, the bass player on the left, in a white jacket with black trim, seems unconcerned, a bystander almost, stock still apart from nimble fingers that rattle off lightning-fast runs with utmost skill and casual precision. The drummer—what you can see of him behind his enormous kit—wears a red T-shirt and blue jeans rolled up to his knees, a blur of strenuous activity, occasionally throwing his sticks into the air and catching them, a flamboyant showman in a sideshow all of his own. From time to time, the guitarist approaches the drummer and they animate one another, finding new energy, new sparks, new inspiration, as they coalesce, their eyes locked together. The singer,

meanwhile, commands center stage, his hair flowing down around his ears in golden curls, bare-chested beneath a long beige suede coat, a garment strewn with tassels that swirl like corals beneath the sea as he throws his microphone into the air, swinging it lasso-style on its cord before catching it and delivering the next vocal line.

The Who's performance includes a forty-minute, nonstop recital of songs from their rock opera, *Tommy*, released as a double long-playing album three months previously. Most members of the audience haven't heard a note of it before tonight, but they've never seen or heard anything like the spectacle up there onstage right now. This British group, to use an expression in vogue at the time, is simply blowing their minds.

Like a classical opera, *Tommy* incorporates recurrent musical themes that become familiar as it is performed, repeated guitar riffs, choruses, and lyrics, and in this way it builds a momentum that the huge audience recognize as something far more profound than what is served up at conventional rock shows by less skilled practitioners in the art of live performance. Other groups play a song, finish it, and then start another. This group is different. No group they've ever seen before connects so many songs—seventeen in all—together virtually uninterrupted like this,[6] or performs with this kind of athleticism, abandon, and dedication to the cause, or puts quite so much effort into their performance yet at the same time manages to sound so controlled, so cohesive, so electrifying. As the opera unfolds, many in the audience recognize recurring motifs and begin to identify with its ideas and with the music. About halfway in, it's starting to become memorable—as if they have heard it all before, but in reality it's all new to them.

right: Daltrey, his coat "strewn with tassels that swirl like corals beneath the sea," onstage at Woodstock. As the oldest member of the group, Daltrey tried—but more often than not failed—to keep the other three from overindulging in alcohol and drugs.

As if by divine intervention, when the rock opera reaches its conclusion, dawn's early light rises behind the group, and thousands upon thousands of new Who fans rise to acknowledge them. But, remarkably, The Who's performance is not yet over. Barely pausing to catch their breath, they launch into a couple of rock 'n' roll standards, performed back to back with maximum swagger, followed by a seven-minute rendering of "My Generation"—"our hymn," as the surly guitarist calls it. At the close, in a gesture of casual disdain for the tools of his trade, the guitarist unplugs his guitar, smashes it onto the stage several times, and then chucks it into the crowd. It has served its purpose and can now be discarded.

The ovation they receive is long and loud, still ringing in their ears as they hop aboard a helicopter that takes them to New York City. The performance onstage and in the subsequent film of the event turns The Who into superstars, brand leaders of the stadium rock explosion waiting just around the corner.

Later, though, all of The Who, especially the guitarist, will say how much they hated Woodstock. "Fucking awful," is their most common observation.

The next show The Who played, on August 22, was at the Market Hall in Shrewsbury in Shropshire, England, where the capacity was just short of one thousand.

opposite: At the start of The Who's June 1968 US tour, they were persuaded by their US record label, Decca, to pose alongside this psychedelic bus in order to promote their single "Magic Bus." To their horror, a photograph from the session was used on the cover of the US LP *Magic Bus: The Who On Tour*, an inferior mix of B-sides and album cuts that was misleadingly titled so as to appear to be a live recording.

above: Festivalgoers relax on the grass near the Meher Baba tent during the Woodstock Music and Arts Fair.

It was billed as an Antiquarian Exposition—three days of peace and music. But it was chaos. And then halfway through the night the organisers decided they weren't going to pay us."

Roger Daltrey, *Thanks a Lot Mr. Kibblewhite: My Story*, 2018

own reflection—a leap forward in the healing process that seamlessly juxtaposes a second refrain of "See Me, Feel Me" with the "Listening to You" coda into the heavier "Mirror" riff. For "Tommy Can You Hear Me," Daltrey leads The Who in a folksy sing-along in virtual unison, accompanied only by Pete's ringing acoustic guitar and John's springy bass, while "Smash the Mirror" is a brief, dramatic snatch highlighted by the ascending "rise, rise, rise" lyrics and the sound of breaking glass. Tommy, it seems, can now hear, speak, and see.

"Sensation," written long before *Tommy* was formulated and sung by Townshend, nevertheless seems appropriate, as does the catchy, lightweight pop rhythm punctuated by Entwistle on French horn. On "Miracle Cure," a newspaper vendor spreads the news of Tommy's rebirth, offering a quick link into "Sally Simpson," which on first hearing sounds as if it belongs on another album entirely. Missing are the rhythmic structures that crop up so often elsewhere, here replaced by a rather thin melody, as befits a narrative song about how Sally, a fan of Tommy, disobeys her father, heads out to see him perform in concert, gets caught up in a crush in front of the stage, and is permanently disfigured as a result.

A memorable six-chord riff introduces "I'm Free," one of the album's more straightforward riff-based rock songs, in which Tommy shares his delight at being cured, throws off the shackles of his handicaps, and urges his followers—those attracted by his prowess at pinball—to follow him. Tinkly piano, a great acoustic solo, and a nice reuse of the familiar "Pinball" intro riff all reinforce a song that, set apart from *Tommy*, became a US single in its own right. "Welcome," which vies with "1921" as the prettiest song on the album, with The

Who at their most melodic, intensifies at its heart, with Daltrey on harmonica, then returns to its mannered, rather dreamy aura. Moon's sole writing credit on *Tommy*, "Tommy's Holiday Camp," follows, offering one minute of Townshend's vocal over a fairground barrel organ extolling the virtues of the holiday camp that Tommy has established as the base for his mission.

Finally, "We're Not Gonna Take It" is two songs in one, the first a catchy, upbeat, riff-based piece about rejecting fascism, the second a circular, looping prayer for unification, the two linked by Tommy's elegiac plea to be seen, felt, touched, and healed—which, in the hands of Daltrey, became as important a motif for the opera as any complete song. With its churning major chords, the finale to *Tommy* that follows is among the simplest yet most effective pieces of music that Townshend has ever written. "See Me, Feel Me," a.k.a. "Listening to You," is the most obvious hymn to Meher Baba—or any deity—in The Who's catalogue, a crystal-clear homage delivered by Tommy to his disciples, and when it was played live, it appeared for all the world as if The Who were paying a remarkable tribute to the audience they were singing to. In this respect, it couldn't fail to lift the spirits—just as all hymns are designed to do.

Listening to Who?

Tommy is not without its flaws. Most of the linking songs are slight; Entwistle's songs grate against those by Townshend; the plot is vague; and, as Dave Marsh observes in his Who biography *Before I Get Old*, Townshend often tries to cram too much into the lyrics. "Almost inevitably, only Townshend—perhaps Lambert and, in some

right: Townshend plays a Fender Electric XII 12-string—an instrument he never used onstage—during the *Tommy* sessions at IBC Studios, October 1968.

cases, one or two of the band members—knew the story that the lyrics were meant to convey," Marsh writes. "Most often, no one outside the group could have guessed."

This explains why Townshend did hundreds of interviews in which he attempted to explain the plot of *Tommy*. "Of course, since the action was sufficiently vague to confuse even Pete from time to time, his explanations were often contradictory, misleading, or simply confusing," writes Marsh. "One of *Tommy*'s purposes was to disseminate the spiritual concepts of Meher Baba as all-too-imperfectly grasped by Townshend. Since those precepts were none too understandable to begin with, much of the opera was a muddle. This engendered further misunderstanding and additional rounds of clarification."

Townshend admitted as much himself, drawing attention to a feature in the *Radio Times* that offered three contradictory theories about the origins of Tommy: Nik Cohn felt it was inspired by his book on a pinball champion; Mike McInnerney believed it was inspired by Meher Baba; and Roger Daltrey felt it all came from Kit Lambert's imagination. A perplexed Townshend would admit, "The point is I don't really know."

The real question is whether or not any of this matters. Literal meaning has never been a prerequisite for a rock song to be considered great, and any ambiguities in the storyline don't detract from the pleasure fans derived from listening to *Tommy* from beginning to end. Neither, at the outset, was *Tommy* intended as a classical opera in which the characters would act out their parts onstage while singing. Perhaps the best description is a "cantata," defined in dictionaries as "a medium-length narrative piece of music for voices with instrumental accompaniment, typically with solos,

chorus, and orchestra." But cantata doesn't have the cachet of "opera," which sounds grand and is certainly more appropriate than "concept album," a term that came into common usage to describe albums with a unifying theme that did not necessarily tell a story, as *Tommy* is designed to do.

"*Tommy* transcends such enigma," I wrote in 1984, in what at the time was the first biography of Pete Townshend to be published. "The strongest songs exist as potential singles outside of the conceptual framework: 'Pinball Wizard' with the most exhilarating guitar part The Who have ever recorded; 'Amazing Journey,' delicate yet driving; 'Christmas,' on which Roger outdistances even his own improving standards; 'Acid Queen,' a malevolent piece for the wickedest witch; 'I'm Free,' a truly great riff; and the closing song, 'We're Not Gonna Take It,' with its hymn-like coda, 'See Me, Feel Me.' The three instrumental pieces, 'Overture,' 'Sparks,' and 'Underture,' are all models of dynamics where Keith Moon, given the freedom to lead, re-establishes himself as the most perfectly equipped drummer in the whole of rock."

I could perhaps have added that more than any other member of The Who, *Tommy* was a career-defining moment for Roger Daltrey, hitherto the least heralded member of the group, and perhaps even the weakest link until now. Everyone already knew that Townshend was a great songwriter and pioneering guitarist; that Entwistle was a superb bass player, as proficient as anyone in this line of work; and that Moon was the most gifted and original drummer of his generation.

Sometime during the recording of *Tommy*, Daltrey realized that the opera gave him an unrivaled opportunity to shine as never before. He sang superbly throughout, be it in rock songs like "Amazing Journey"

or "Pinball" or on delicate numbers like "Welcome," and, most notably, the key lines that introduce the "Listening to You" coda of "We're Not Gonna Take It." In these lines—"See me, feel me, touch me, heal me," repeated four times—Daltrey really did *become* Tommy, although, ironically, it was Kit Lambert's initial intention to have Townshend sing these lines, as he did most of the delicate passages in the opera.

"There was an extraordinary moment in the recording of *Tommy*," Townshend recalled of these lines in the documentary *Sensation: The Story of Tommy*. "I arrived late, looking forward to doing my bit, which was singing the emotional bits. Roger had had a couple of goes and Kit was going, 'I don't think you'd better do this Rog, you'd better leave this to Pete,' and I came in and I heard [Daltrey singing

'See Me, Feel Me'] . . . and I realized that Roger had occupied Tommy in such a way that other people weren't able to occupy him."

"I was inhabiting the music," Daltrey added. "I think everybody has a longing in them to be understood, to be loved, and that's what I tried to do." In concert, as we shall see, Daltrey actually became Tommy in the eyes of The Who's audiences. His characterization—which would eventually lead to a second career as an actor—of the deaf, dumb, and blind boy brought Townshend's opera to life, and gave it a depth that must have astounded even its writer. Within twelve months of the album's release, Roger Daltrey's portrayal of Tommy had turned him into one of the world's great rock singers, sexy, assured, and commanding—the archetype blueprint of the rock god personified.

opposite: Realizing that *Tommy* offered him an unprecedented opportunity, Daltrey relished recording its songs. "I was inhabiting the music," he later said.

right: A press advert for *Tommy* that utilizes the same image of Townshend that was used to promote The Who's legendary Marquee shows, which ran from November 1964 to April 1965.

'tommy'

The who

TRACK RECORD 613 013/4

I think *Tommy* is reflective of the mood of a generation. It's one where the see-saw has been over heavy at one end for too long, and youth is now at the point where it has to make the decision . . . I think it is going the right way, and that there is a real mental revolution taking place in the minds of these young people and one step nearer the spiritual revolution which will follow."

Pete Townshend to *Record Mirror*, December 13, 1969

opposite: Daltrey on *Top of the Pops*, promoting "Pinball Wizard," the first single to be taken from *Tommy* in March 1969. Moon's behavior that day resulted in a comical exchange of letters to the effect that The Who could appear on *TOTP* in future only if their drummer was sober.

The Final Step

By and large, the reviews for *Tommy* were almost unanimously positive. Nik Cohn was as good as his word, writing in the *New York Times*, "*Tommy* is just possibly the most important work that anyone has yet done in rock. This might just be the first pop masterpiece." In *Life* magazine, Albert Goldman was equally effusive, concluding that the album "outstrips anything that has ever come out of a rock recording studio . . . every one of *Tommy*'s twenty-five tracks offers something memorable. Which makes this pinball opera, all slamming jolts and gidget chatter, the heaviest score of the rock generation."

In the *International Times*, the UK's leading underground paper, Miles wrote, "It is impossible to praise this album too highly. As progressive pop music has edged further and further along the limb . . . certain groups have appeared in the vanguard, notably The Beatles starting with *Sgt. Pepper* and The Mothers with *Uncle Meat*. The final step, however, has been taken by The Who with a full-scale pop opera. Even more important is that this is not a tentative step— *Tommy* is solid and strong and integrated throughout from the first bold statements of theme on the French horn to the slow fadeout of the almost holy final soliloquy."

In *Record Mirror*, Lon Goddard gave the album a five-star rating and wrote, "This has got to be one of the most incredible feats ever accomplished in music. The subject is Tommy, the boy who saw his mother pollenating the wrong flower, which caused him to go deaf, dumb and blind with shock. [The Who] have managed to create a number of different moods throughout the opera and used all facets of the power spectrum, from the heaviest and loudest to the gentle and the subtle; in fact, all the ingredients needed to classify it a fine opera."

An uncredited writer in *Melody Maker* commented that the two-album set would "add great prestige to the recording industry and pop scene alike." The writer also downplayed any suggestions that *Tommy* was in any way in bad taste or even obscene, claiming that, "If anything, it is extremely tasteful in its treatment of very real situations. . . . In four sides the music covers a variety of moods from coarse excitement to crystal beauty." This variety was attributed to "Kit Lambert's production, and the Who's instrumental ability . . . Pete's guitar work is heard at its best ever, especially on the 'Overture' and the half-time instrumental 'Underture.' Roger Daltrey sings with great care and conviction throughout, and Keith Moon's drumming is as vital and invaluable as ever. Let us hope the success of *Tommy* will spur Pete quickly on to the next project."

Only the *New Musical Express* cast doubt on the project, with Allen Evans writing, "Admittedly the idea is original, even though other groups seem to be jumping on the bandwagon now, but it doesn't come off. Pretentious is too strong a word: maybe ambitious is the right term, but sick certainly does apply."

None of this really mattered one iota. *Tommy* went to #2 in the British album charts and #4 in the United States. It sold two hundred thousand copies in the first two weeks in the US alone, and by the middle of August it was awarded a gold disc for sales in excess of five hundred thousand. More importantly, it rescued The Who from oblivion, turned them into superstars, and ensured their reputation for all time.

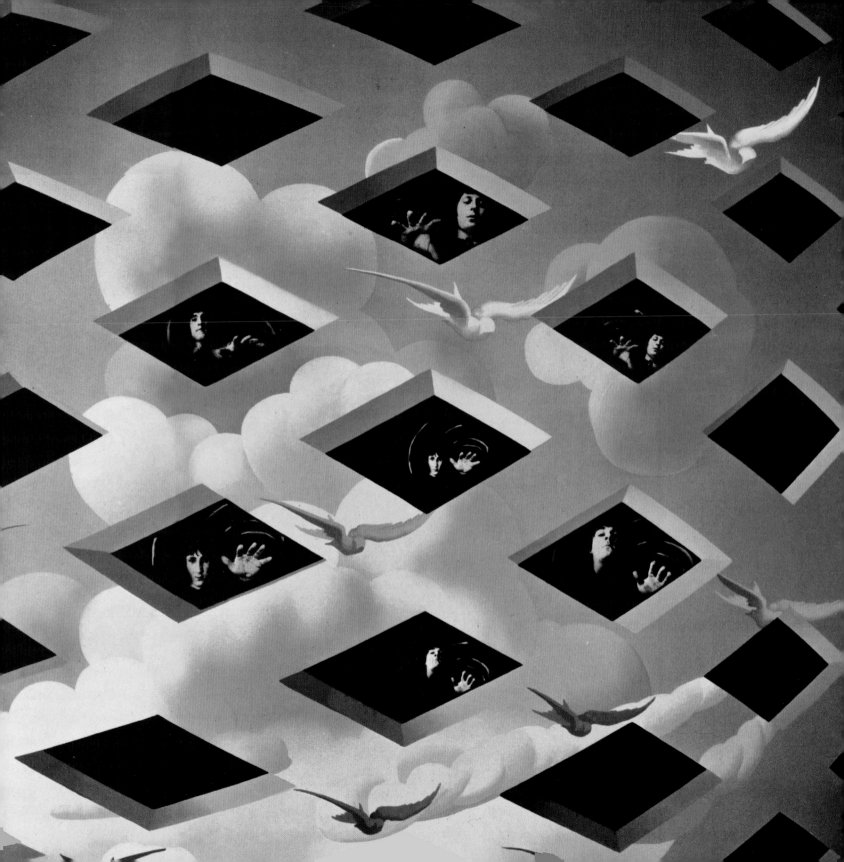

3 the look

Mike McInnerney

the look

Pete and I were beneficiaries of a well-established British art-school system. Art and design schools in London and across the United Kingdom were undergoing a shakeup at the time, thanks to the 1961 Coldstream Report, which recommended changing the emphasis of art and design education so that it served the needs of Britain's expanding design and communications industry more effectively. The report also recommended granting a more broadly based art and design award status equivalent to a university degree, with stricter entry requirements. The new award—the Diploma in Art and Design, or DipAD—would have positive consequences for future practice, for both students and teachers, though some had reservations.[7]

It was not until 1964 that I could afford to study, and I applied to the London College of Printing (now London College of Communication). I had left school at sixteen and worked in advertising until 1964, the year that Harold Wilson's new Labour government resolved to implement the Robbins Report's recommendations of 1963. As well as expanding the number of universities, the report aimed to encourage more working-class students to go to university. As a working-class boy, I was now eligible, subject to qualifications and acceptance, to a full fee and generous maintenance grant—there was no need to apply for one of the limited number of local authority discretionary awards and county scholarships available at the time. I was interviewed at the LCP by Tom Eckersley, head of the graphic design department, and offered a place on the pre-diploma course.

In the autumn of 1964, the London College of Printing was one of twenty-nine British art and design colleges allowed to run the Diploma in Art and Design courses. I entered as the first intake for the new award, which was undergoing the teething problems that usually accompany the implementation of new practices. The LCP's design curriculum was influenced by the basic design course, made common for both fine art and design students, devised by Victor Pasmore and Richard Hamilton at the Fine Art Department of King's College, Newcastle-upon-Tyne. Modernism was the established orthodoxy for most students of design in 1964, and Pasmore and Hamilton in turn had been influenced by postwar basic design ideas developed by the Vorkurs program started by Johannes Itten at Walter Gropius' famed Bauhaus school, which was founded in 1919 in Weimar Germany. The Vorkurs programs taught students to take a rational approach when making art—rather than replicating nature, or creating representational art, students were encouraged to understand qualities of line, pattern, and form and their interaction, when freed of content.

Roy Ascot, who established the new foundation course at Ealing Art College in 1961, had studied under Pasmore and Hamilton at Newcastle. His interest in the notion of art as process and the relationship between the artist, the artwork, and society at large would lead to a focus on *doing* rather than any interest in the finished artwork. For example, the nature of drawing was questioned in a number of exercises which set strict parameters, as in the case of a project defined as "time-drawing" of the model: "Draw her hair in three seconds, face in three minutes, left hand thumb nail in three hours, legs in six seconds, right ankle in two days." He would create activities and exercises that deliberately forced students to question

previous spread: A detail from the *Tommy* record cover featuring portraits of The Who—a last-minute insertion required by Decca for release into the North American market.

top right: The Who in pop-art gear, photographed backstage at a concert in Amsterdam, the Netherlands, in September 1965.

bottom right: Victor Pasmore (*left*) explains an abstract artwork to Tate Gallery director Norman Reid and a group of students, May 13, 1965.

left: *The Climax*, an 1893 line block print by Aubrey Beardsley, whose work influenced the psychedelic movement when it was exhibited at the Victoria and Albert Museum in London in 1966.

right: Granny Takes a Trip: one of a range of storefront facades created for the first psychedelic boutique in London, as founded by Nigel Waymouth, Sheila Cohen, and John Pearse at 488 Kings Road in 1966.

their assumptions and preconceptions of practice in his famous "groundcourse," which was delivered to all first year students, including Pete Townshend. Ascot was part of the transition between traditional and new ideas of teaching, with new developments in art practice and in popular culture prominent in the sixties via installation art, performance art, pop art, op art, computer art, conceptual art, music, poetry, theater, fashion, and film.

Pete entered Ealing College of Art in 1961, just when this revolutionary period in the teaching and practice of art was beginning. Pete was introduced to Dadaism, and to Dadaist ideas of re-appropriation, to mixed-media experience, and to techniques such as collage, alongside the Fluxus-inspired art performance of Gustav Metzger (who would influence Pete's guitar-smashing stage performances). Contemporary ideas on art practice and multi-discipline performance were delivered through visiting lecturers such as painters Larry Rivers and R. B. Kitaj and sculptor Brian Wall.

Pete's art school experience would have a long-term effect on The Who and the way they evolved artistically in terms of visual presence and stage performance, as well as the way they crafted their songs and introduced sonic ideas such as feedback alongside the application of new recording techniques. The "pop" images that branded The Who—the targets, arrows, and chevrons, and most famously the wearing of the British Union Jack—came out of his art-college training. It is what distinguished The Who from rival bands such as The Kinks and Small Faces.

During my time at the London College of Printing, I became interested in developing my drawing and painting skills within the discipline of illustration, which were not on the curriculum. There was little opportunity to explore an emotional and subjective voice in my work, or to pursue personal interests, except for a course on perception, which came via visiting lecturers and complementary studies.

My escape from the ruling modernist ethos came via London's emerging political and creative counterculture. The new scene offered an atmosphere of discussion and opportunity, particularly in my London neighborhood of Notting Hill Gate. I was able to contribute to a developing visual language expressing personal experiences of psychotropic drugs in this alternative society.

The new counterculture scene provided an alternative world of ornament and pattern in search of new aesthetics. All of a sudden, ideas were released from the shackles of modernism with liberating thoughts of prettiness, beautifulness, lushness, and delirious, exotic playfulness, happily borrowing motifs from the turn-of-the-century Art Nouveau (or *Jugendstil*) aesthetic as expressed in the sinuous line of Aubrey Beardsley drawings and curvilinear patterns of Alphonse Mucha posters.

Pattern entered the scene, too, creating a backdrop for the Summer of Love—pattern as a pastoral poem for urban hippie sentiments with a bucolic Englishness and fairytale quality, as William Morris wallpaper spread across apartment walls and onto men's outfits courtesy of the Granny Takes a Trip boutique. I would share doodle games with friends and play with automatic drawing that referenced early psychedelic light shows. I cultivated an interest in soft, fluid, melting, liquid abstract forms and the patterned illusions of optical art, then part of the contemporary art scene.

hems and fringes
a conversation with karen townshend

In the early 1960s, Karen Astley, the daughter of television score composer Edwin Astley, enrolled at Ealing Art College, where she studied art and textiles. While there, she met her future husband, Pete Townshend. Here, Karen recalls her time at Ealing and with Pete in a conversation with Mike McInnerney and *Gramophone* magazine art editor Dinah Lone.

Mike McInnerney: Why did you choose Ealing Art College?

Karen Townshend: Not a very interesting reason, I'm afraid. At school, the art teacher was very encouraging to me, and she suggested that as I liked art I should go to drawing classes on Saturday mornings at Ealing. I went when I was sixteen—I did an art A-level, and then dress design and pattern cutting, and then a City and Guilds [vocational apprenticeship].

MM: Were you aware of any new teaching methods at Ealing?

KT: No, because they did not do that in the dress department. I always got the impression things were badly organized—that people did not know what they were doing, and were left to their own devices an incredible amount.

One time, Roy Ascot decided he wanted some of the fashion students to experience the "groundcourse," and some of those who had five O-levels—it turned out not everybody did—were allowed to go and be part of it on Wednesday afternoons . . . and then he sort of left the room, and we didn't do anything because we did not know what he was talking about.

MM: Richard Barnes says the influences came more from the visiting lecturers.

KT: Yes, I think that is what Pete would say, too, because he often talked about Ron Kitaj coming, and about Gustav Metzger.

I never remember seeing work on walls. Pete has told the story many times of going to a class and being told to start by drawing a line, and everyone had to practice drawing a line without using a ruler, and then they went to the next class and were told first to throw everything you know about drawing a line out of the window—you have to do it some other way entirely.

It was really confusing, because you did not know the [parameters]. There was an awful lot of talk about cybernetics, and I don't think anyone knew what it meant, really. And yet it seems to be universally believed that there was a great flowering of the art school in the sixties, and that British creativity is all about what came out of those art schools. I don't know how it happened!

Dinah Lone: Probably because it gave people more space to do something else.

KT: You didn't have to be there all day.

DL: What was the dress design department aiming to do with their students—to put you out into the industry?

KT: Annie [Duprée] got a pattern-cutting job; another student went to work with Mary Quant. I don't remember anybody going to do a degree somewhere else. I left before the third year, when I was eighteen.

MM: That's when you began working with the people from Hem and Fringe. Where did Annie Duprée and Angela Brown first set up?

right: Pete Townshend with sewing machine during a photo session at his mother Betty's antique shop, Miscellanea, on Ealing Common, October 8, 1966.

KT: Somewhere in Pimlico—it was at some hairdresser's, which is why it's got a strange name. A boutique.

MM: Did you know Michael Rainey, the fashion designer?

KT: A bit, yes. Through the making of shirts. We were making those at the flat on Eccleston Square, and before that in Princedale Road, where Angela lived with Michael English. Angela and I were making stuff at Princedale Road, and Michael was working with Nigel Waymouth. They lived in one room, Michael and Angela—everything in one room. We had a sewing machine, and I think Michael was working in the same room.

 We made lots of things out of Indian bedspreads. There was a store in Kensington called Pontings, which had wonderful old-fashioned fabric. They had all the slipper satin in beautiful pastel colors that we [used to make] a particular little kind of sleeveless dress that was screen-printed with an *art nouveau* print down one side, then we just put some sequins around some of the curves, each one a bit different. We made lots of those, lots of Indian dresses.

MM: When you moved from Ebury Street to Twickenham in 1968, how did you find it? This is a question linked to how Baba came into your life . . .

KT: I never quite "got it" to the extent that you did. But it was lovely, especially with you and Katie living down the road, and then Ronnie and Sue [Lane] turned up.

MM: It grew as a community.

KT: Nobody had a normal job, so there were people you could go to see. Walk along the embankment with baby Emma [Pete and Karen's daughter, born in March 1969] in the pram and know there was somebody at home—Mike at his desk endlessly.

MM: Even when someone like you wasn't directly as interested, as a follower of Baba, there was something about the people that was very attractive. Which may have brought everyone together, to be in that area.

KT: It did. You moved to Richmond to be close to Delia, didn't you? Pete and I were just looking for a house. We quite fancied living on the river, but we'd just looked at a house in Maidenhead. By pure chance, a house came up for sale on the Embankment, by the river in Twickenham.

MM: Then not much time for you as a couple to settle . . .

KT: That was what things were like at that time [in 1968]. When I think about what happened—it was Pete's birthday in May; we got married the next day; then it was my twenty-first; then we got a dog; then the day after we got married we bought a house at auction; then, in mid-June, we moved into it; then Pete went on a very long US tour and came back to enter the studio to record *Tommy*. That's just insane, isn't it?

MM: Richard Barnes mentions that he and Pete lived in this separate art-school world, away from the rest of the band. At Embankment, I was never really aware of Roger, John, or Keith being part of what one might call a day-to-day friendship. I don't know if it was because it was a "Baba bubble," but moving from a counterculture community to Twickenham was like another country, very self-contained.

KT: I don't think Pete ever was very good friends with anyone in The Who. I think he was friends with John at school, but I don't think Pete would ever have thought of himself as friends with Roger. But he did used to socialize with John a bit. And you had things going on as well, at Willoughby House, with garden parties and what have you. So I think there was quite a lot of being sociable.

left: The auto-destructive artist Gustav Metzger experiments with acid on nylon in a public performance of his *Acid Action Painting*, 1961.

This play with drawing contributed to the vocabulary of forms used to create images for posters I produced for the scene at the time. Swirling psychedelic patterns of liquid light shows reinforced altered states and the synesthesia of sonic and visual experience. Listening to music on acid seemed to encourage an ear for sounds, creating mood and groove like the drone of a sitar or prolonged rhythms, patterns and repetitions of minimalist music by John Cage and Terry Riley, the patterned guitar work of John Fahey, and the seamless improvised jazz piano of Keith Jarrett.

My developing interest in the spiritual teachings of Meher Baba reintroduced a college involvement with perception and spatial illusion created by patterns of op art (short for optical art) that questioned how we view things. The Necker cube trickery of M. C. Escher confused the eye and brain in its attempt to make perceptual sense of uncertain viewpoints; the mathematical rhymes and rhythms of Islamic tiles and their sacred geometry echoed nature's symmetry and provided inspiration for the organization of my pictorial ideas. The compressed intensity of LSD experience brought a passionate concentration to looking at the most ordinary things, from rainbow patterns on soap bubbles to the pattern of brick walls observed on occasional psychotropic trips through London. Pattern was everywhere.

A Physical Decade

The sixties was a physical decade; a decade that saw humankind escape Earth's gravity to land on the Moon. The Who were a very physical band, too, and *Tommy* a physical story—an epiphany of

the senses. The epoch highlighted a world of sound, sight, touch, taste, and smell experienced through the culture of science, art, politics, and technology. Senses would inform notions of expression in art, theater, dance, music, cinema, performance, and poetry. A new generation explored heightened senses through use of drugs. The subject of illusion and perception created cultural themes; stage performances of hypnotism and magic grew more popular, and research into perception explored the physiology and psychology of eye and brain.

The art performances of Gustav Metzger—which included the spraying of acid onto sheets of nylon, producing rapidly changing shapes in the dissolving nylon—were considered both auto-destructive and auto-creative. In his 1967 interview with Barry Miles for *International Times*, Pete said of Metzger, "Nobody knew what it was all about. Before The Who got big, I wanted them to get bigger and bigger and bigger until a number-one record, and then wrap dynamite round their heads and blow themselves up on TV . . . well-presented destruction is what I call a joy to watch, just like well presented pornography or obscenity. . . . I'd always thought that high-class, high-powered auto-destructive art, glossy destruction, glossy pop destruction, was far, far better than the terrible messy, dirty disorganized destruction that other people were involved in."

In Britain, performance poetry grew in popularity during the sixties as poets used their voices to deliver words off the page and into the audience. The International Poetry Incarnation at the Royal Albert Hall was a mass celebration of performance poetry in front of a

above: Townshend smashes his guitar into Marshall speaker cabinets at the climax of The Who's appearance at the Windsor Jazz and Blues Festival, July 30, 1966.

❝ Music is vibrations, vibrations of the soul, of the air. It's a whole means of communicating to your other extensions, which is the audience. But audiences don't really know why they are there. They might come to see you break a guitar or something like that . . . ❞

Pete Townshend to the *Village Voice*, April 11, 1968

above: Choreographer Merce Cunningham and composer John Cage, photographed together prior to a performance in New London, Connecticut, August 1963.

right: *A Quick One*, The Who's second LP, was released in December 1966 and featured cover artwork by Alan Aldridge, who would later design the sleeve for Elton John's 1975 album *Captain Fantastic and the Brown Dirt Cowboy*.

nascent counterculture audience of seven thousand people on June 11, 1965. In the United States, the artist Robert Rauschenberg, composer John Cage, and choreographer Merce Cunningham would highlight creative process by drawing attention to the experience of mark-making as the grammar of drawing, sound as the grammar of music, and movement as the grammar of dance

in their collaborative performances. In dance, Pina Bausch also created extraordinary physical choreography that could involve stumbling, crashing, and dancing with your eyes closed. An experimental troupe of performers called the Living Theatre—a US stage company founded by actress Judith Malina and painter/poet Julian Beck—would confront audience complacency through physical theatre, direct spectacle, and audience participation.

Richard Long, sculptor student at St Martins School of Art, London would expend a lot of effort walking back and forth across a grassy field in Wiltshire to create a transient line in nature for his 1967 piece titled "A Line Made by Walking." London-based artist John Latham lost his St. Martins School of Art teaching post in 1966 when he chewed up a library copy of Clement Greenberg's *Art and Culture* and returned the book's "essence" as a phial of fermented spit. In 1968, the artist Christo wrapped the Kunsthalle in Bern, Germany, turning art into event.

By the end of the sixties, art had begun to dematerialize into conceptual practice; it became less about physicality and more about "the idea," a development highlighted in the radical landmark 1969 Kunsthalle exhibition Live in Your Head: When Attitude Becomes Form.

Out of the Blue

My commission to produce artwork for the new Who album, provisionally titled *Deaf, Dumb, and Blind Boy*, came as a surprise. In the middle of September 1968, Pete and the band entered IBC Studios at 35 Portland Place, opposite the BBC's Broadcasting House, to start recording the album. One morning in late September, Pete took a detour from his house by the Thames in Twickenham, on his way to IBC, and popped into my studio at Willoughby House with a breathtaking offer for me to create packaging for his new opera.

Pete had originally considered commissioning Alan Aldridge to design the cover artwork, Aldridge having previously created the sleeve for The Who's 1966 album *A Quick One*, using his signature psychedelic cartoon style to depict the four members of the band. Pete had moved on since then, however; pop songs that referenced his own personal history were now becoming rock songs with larger themes and stories that would carry more demanding musical ideas, purpose, and meaning under the influence of Meher Baba's teachings. He would discuss ideas such as these with others as they took shape, as he did in an interview with Jann Wenner of *Rolling Stone*, published in the magazine's issue dated September 14, 1968.

It was around this time that Pete's story of a human journey became one of a *seeker*. I was part of that talking-out process, which made me possibly the best candidate to help articulate these ideas in a visual form that would make sense of the project's link to Baba.

I was concerned about how much time I'd be afforded to create artwork when Pete first spoke to me in late September, at which point the plan was to release the album for the Christmas market.

seeing is believing
sense-based knowledge

Sense-based knowledge was a popular area of exploration in the sixties, when investigations into the psychology of seeing and the mechanics of perception were explored through studies of the brain.

The psychologist Richard L. Gregory investigated the senses—especially sight and hearing—and how they work in his bestseller *Eye and Brain: The Psychology of Seeing* published in 1966. The book describes how we see brightness, movement, color, and objects. Visual illusions are used to establish principles about how perception normally works and sometimes fails. When you are looking, you are using experience to make sense of what you see, based on previous understandings. If what you see is unknown, you may try an educated guess—an opinion on what you believe is true based on what you know and observe to form a conclusion about something (conjecture).

Two examples were used in perception tests at the time to illustrate these assumptions. They measured mind distraction and brain action in relation to recognition. The first is the classic reversible figure and ground illusion, a black-and-white picture that never really settles, seen at one moment as two facing profiles and another moment as the outline of a vase. The second measure is the Necker cube, which contains no depth cues, and which in turn leads to ambiguity as the brain attempts to make perceptual sense of a cube seen both from the top and the bottom at the same time.

The perception-altering effects of LSD and psilocybin fungi heightened the sense-based experience of the sixties. These psychotropic substances seemed to coordinate mood, apparently allowing connections to form between regions of the brain that rarely communicate with each other. They enabled people to transform the way they perceive the world, and, in some cases, helped the treatment of depression and anxiety in those resistant to standard treatment. The drugs activate serotonin receptors, which triggers the illusions and hallucinations that create the "trippy," bizarre visual effects they are known for. Tests carried out on hallucinogens by the US military in the late fifties and early sixties identified a visual and sonic vocabulary later used as psychedelic aesthetic by the counterculture, leading to a focus on repetition and pattern; perceptual distortions such as fluctuations in the apparent size, shape, color, distance, and texture of surfaces; as well as synesthesia, kaleidoscopic imagery, and hallucinations.

In the sixties, the op art movement developed perceptual ideas in the form of painting and sculpture. Bridget Riley's black-and-white optical work produced between 1961 and '64 uses a variety of geometric forms to produce sensations of movement or color. In "Movement in Squares," a simple constant line of narrowing squares persuades the eye to fall into the bending dip created by the illusion. Riley was herself influenced by Georges Seurat, the neoimpressionist who in the late nineteenth century created a new way of seeing the world as a field of colored dots. Using a technique called pointillism, he relied on the eye to complete the color mix created by the controlled application of points of color.

Color is the most powerful illusion nature plays on us. We see the same colors when hard-wired by evolution, but color shaped by individual experience and how we feel is a separate phenomenon. Single-cell organisms in the oceans harvest energy from the longer wavelengths of orange, yellow, and red but avoid the damaging lethal ultraviolet rays of the sun. The eye does not simply see color; the brain creates it based on the knowledge of what things should

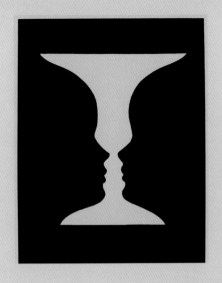

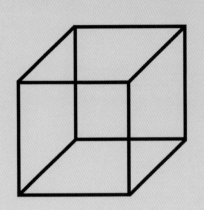

look like. Forty million years ago, red and green receptors were added to the vocabulary of communication in the elaborate color systems of nature in order to read warning signs and the color of fruit. Words learned may impact how the brain processes color. English has twelve color categories; the Himba tribe in northern Namibia has five color categories and uses the same word for green and blue. The Welsh language has no word for pink or brown; the closest welsh word to pink is *gwyngoch*, which means white-red.

A simple test is to try and think about and hold a mental image of a color. Most people should be able to mentally see the colors that appear in the basic primary, secondary, and tertiary color wheel: red, yellow, blue / green, orange, purple / green-yellow, yellow-orange, orange-red, red–violet / violet-blue / blue-green . . . after that it becomes tricky. The human eye can in fact distinguish ten million different hues (colors or shade of color), but only through the visual act of comparison.

top left: A reversible figure and ground illusion. The image never settles—one moment it is viewed as two face profiles, the next as a vase.

bottom left: The Necker cube provides no depth cues, leading to ambiguity as the brain attempts to make perceptual sense of a cube seen both from the top and bottom at the same time.

above right: A pattern of black and white concentric lines creates, through the precise manipulation of width from negative to positive, an illusion that tricks the brain into seeing 3D tonal waves.

Fortunately, the recording of the album was taking longer than expected. The Who needed funds to pay for the sessions, so had taken to working Monday through Thursday in the studio and playing concerts around the country on weekends in order to feed cash into the project. In addition, a tour had been arranged for November, so recording had to stop completely for two weeks.

Further delays were created by Pete's ongoing efforts to define the album concept. He would often return home to write and demo new material, which he would then audition to the band the following morning. Some of this new material would come through discussions he and I had as visual ideas developed on packaging for the album. He would then supply me with raw demos on tape to play as I proceeded with image ideas. As *Melody Maker* reporter Chris Welch commented, when visiting the IBC studios in November '68, "There was still no title or coherent plot line for the album."

This was music to my ears. This extra time provided space for the album artwork to expand from a double gatefold LP to a two-fold-open triple package. The concept referenced religious triptychs painted on open-hinged panels, positioned as altarpieces to focus the act of prayer in churches. The expanded packaging idea would carry a visual illusion and hint at the spiritual nature of the project. Band manager Kit Lambert and Pete were very supportive as the original brief expanded from a 24 x 12 inch cover to a 36 x 12 inch cover with a twelve-page booklet highlighting key moments in the libretto.

Pete and Kit Lambert were my only contacts during the making of *Tommy*. My developing friendship with Pete and Karen within the growing Baba community created a world separate from that of

The Who, though I would meet Roger, John, and Keith occasionally, usually at weddings or other events linked to the group. My working relationship with Pete and Kit was informal. Pete was happy to leave plenty of space for me to get on with cover ideas and artwork. I made one or two visits to the IBC studios to hear work in progress, but mostly we would hold casual meetings in the studio at Willoughby House to discuss evolving visual thoughts on the cover, where Pete would report on developments at IBC accompanied by cassettes that included occasional raw demos from his home studio.

Kit would keep in touch by phone with updates on the overall schedule, often asking how things were progressing in what he called my "garret" studio, his assumption being that I was a starving artist living in a cramped living space at the top of a poorly maintained residential building—a reference straight out of Puccini's opera *La bohème*. Kit was very excited by the project, and often shared with me his thoughts on elevating The Who's opera into a high art event. He subsequently created a numbered limited edition for the launch edition of *Tommy*, similar to fine-art prints exhibited in galleries.

The sense that this was a special project meant that as the artwork concepts expanded, so did the fee. I was ultimately paid £1,000 for the artwork—around $2,400 at the time. This was a high fee in the day, considering that Peter Blake and Jann Haworth had received £200 for the *Sgt. Pepper* artwork in 1967. By the time recording was finally finished, on March 7, 1969, the *Deaf, Dumb, and Blind Boy* rock opera had been renamed *Tommy*—an allusion to Tommy Atkins, itself slang for a common soldier in the British Army, and a propaganda character created as heroic symbol in World War I.

❝ I would be in my home studio with my guitar and my tape machine, possibly with a baby crying in the distance, possibly with my beautiful wife lying in bed wondering where I was, thinking, *We've got an album to make in three weeks—and between now and then, I've got to write the songs and we've got eight gigs.*"

Pete Townshend to *The Guardian*, October 8, 2012

left: *La fenêtre rose*: lithographic poster for a psychedelic concert in Paris, November 1967. Created by OMtentacle design duo Mike McInnerney and Dudley Edwards. The client, John Esam, changed the concert title after the image was completed.

above: A photograph of McInnerney in his studio at Willoughby House, as used in Alan Jones's "Disc Gossip" column report on the *New Musical Express* Awards, *Hull Times*, March 6, 1970.

A World Without Senses

The initial ideas for the *Tommy* cover stemmed from my interest in perception and in formalized natural forms in Islamic pattern and other geometric forms. These were interests I had also expressed in work for the Flying Dragon teahouse, and in the poster for the concert *La fenêtre rose*, which was produced during the short life of the OMtentacle partnership with Dudley Edwards, established to promote spiritual ideas and the teachings of Meher Baba.

Illusion was central to the thoughts I had about the Tommy character; illusion and how our senses enhance it. It is hard to imagine a world without senses, just as it is hard to be certain about a world constructed through the senses we use. Sight, sound, touch, taste, and smell, as well as feeling, are the senses used to create individual ideas of the world: impressions of the world we either agree or disagree on; impressions that are at best transitory, changing as we discover new perspectives, or edit what to notice and what not to notice, how we choose to see as ideas of beauty change, how to hear as new sounds are created and what fashion dictates.

Senses are applied every day; they suffer from casual use, leading to automatic actions and thoughtless behavior. Notions of prejudice and narrow definitions of taste are formed through the senses. When a sense is missing, ghost memories can sometimes be produced to compensate lost function. For some people, senses overlap; color can be tasted and sound becomes a smell. Impressions made through the senses are, by definition, transitory, and not really thought through; they gather in the individual as *sanskaras* or physiological impressions; as Meher Baba points out, the very things that can define us as well

as the very things that will also bind us. The hard business of a spiritual journey is about managing the illusion created by *sanskaras* and leaving them behind as we begin to see what is real.

Senses became a popular topic of conversation between Pete and me as the opera developed. Trying to imagine the world Tommy exists in, and how he constructs that world is difficult. It is not possible to close your eyes, plug your ears, close your mouth, and pretend you are in that world. But the mental world of *Tommy* must in some way create unique conditions, providing a very singular idea of self. There is an argument that what we see of the world is made through the mind; that the mind does not passively mirror reality, but that reality conforms to active concepts formed by the mind to conceive it.

Pete saw the sensory deprivation of the central character as a metaphor for spiritual isolation. In *Who I Am*, he writes of how, with the Tommy character, "I was attempting two ambitious stunts at once . . . to describe the disciple–master relationship, and, in a Hermann Hesse–style saga of reincarnation, to connect the seven journeys involving rebirth in an operatic drama that ended in spiritual perfection." In so doing, he borrowed from Baba's teachings. "Each time the child/disciple Tommy is reborn, he returns with new inner wisdom, but still his life is full of struggle. Since the boy's ignorance of his spiritual growth is a kind of disability . . . I decided my deaf, dumb, and blind hero could be autistic. This way, when I wanted to demonstrate the glorious moment of his God-realization, I could simply restore to my hero the use of his senses." In that regard, the character's sensory deprivation would become "a symbol of our own everyday spiritual isolation."

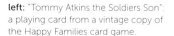

left: "Tommy Atkins the Soldiers Son": a playing card from a vintage copy of the Happy Families card game.

I liked the "idea" of the Tommy character. Rather than trying to portray him, I wanted to picture his experience of being in a world without senses. I think Pete considered him in the early part of the opera as a surface on which people could write their own needs and beliefs. In one of the interviews quoted in *The Who on The Who*, edited by Sean Egan, Pete mentions the Uncle Ernie character becoming loveable because he is so human. "I wanted Tommy to be very remote up to the point where he actually first gets a buzz, and, when he becomes a very remote spiritual figure, kind of saintly."

In the same interview, when asked if he had been purposely withholding information about Tommy, he replied, "Yes. Mike McInnerney and I made a decision in the artwork, too, that we must be very careful not to represent him visually. I shied away from songs in which he spoke . . . originally, 'Sensation' ran, 'He overwhelms as he approaches,' but I felt he really needed to assert himself . . . because he was going to play such a powerful role later on."

How we are in the world is mostly described by sighted people with most of their senses operating. I thought living in Tommy's head would be limitless and unbounded, yet he would be trapped in an environment made for people who have all their senses. The "outer" and "inner" covers of the album seemed like the appropriate place to position this contradiction. The cover uses a reversible figure and ground illusion, an example of perception tests used to measure mind distraction and brain action in relation to recognition. The most famous example is a black-and-white drawing, an unstable image seen as two head profiles at one moment and a vase the next, the brain never settling on one or the other.

For *Tommy*, the closed outer cover presents a blue sky perceived as endless and spacious, limitless and unbounded, across which solid black forms seem to float. Open the two wings of the outer cover and the triptych reveals the blue limitless sky as a shallow surface, a hollow globe representing both Earth and self in limited form floating in an infinite black cosmic space—a space that can never be touched, only imagined in the mind of Tommy. In this limitless space is an image of a hand pointing back at the viewer. The sign, borrowed from a well-known World War I recruitment poster, points back at "you" as an analogy for an individual's personal responsibility for their own spiritual journey.

In contrast to the illusions of space implied on the front cover, the inner cover, with its wall and faux-vintage light fittings, is a symbol of domestic space—the room we all live in, where artificial light illuminates the dark, and where we express our taste for living. I considered the light sconces to be an example of poor taste; they came from sketches made at my mother-in-law's home, and I used them as a critique of her taste in home furnishing. (An attitude that perhaps says something about me and my visual prejudices.)

The light from these fixtures does not fix things as it would in the physical space of the sighted world; here, sunlight gradates into artificial light and then into the imagined space of Tommy's darkness, where light holds no meaning. The final image on the inner sleeve offers a glimpse of nature as seen through the grilles of a window that can be viewed as both flat and as a cube seen from both the top and bottom at the same time—a basic visual-perception trick based on the Necker cube.

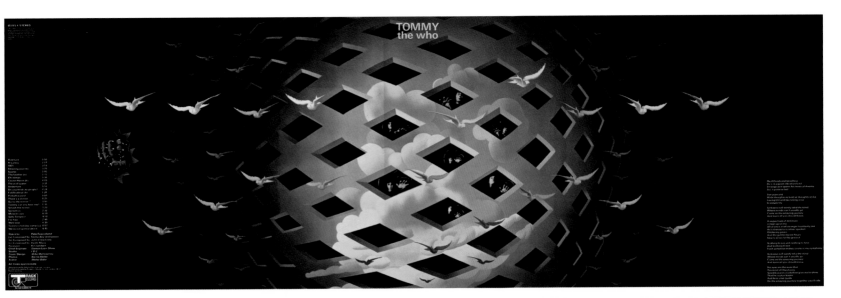

top: The fully extended triptych *Tommy* album cover, with portraits of the band members squeezed into the mesh design at the request of The Who's record label, Decca. All of the *Tommy* artwork was painted in gouache on heavy cartridge paper.

bottom: *Tommy*'s inside cover. A double pocket fold was constructed to contain the album in the last third of the cover, which is illustrated with the facets/birds image.

from mods to rock gods
the changing look of the band

During the sixties, The Who's music went through a series of evolutionary changes, from the brash urgency of "I Can't Explain" and "My Generation" to the multilayered explorations of "Underture" and "We're Not Gonna Take It." The band's image underwent a similar transformation, from sharp mod suits to tie-dye shirts and Union Jack jackets and beyond.

below left: The Who as sharp mods, as shown in a photo session from around March 1965.

below right: Posing in front of Roger's new Volvo at the Duke of York's Barracks, Chelsea, November 12, 1966.

opposite top left: "Hands out" photo session by Tom Wright, taken during The Who's first US tour, August 1967.

opposite top right: The Who standing in the Black Forest, Germany, April 1967.

opposite bottom left: Looking moody in a photo session from June 1968, around the time of the "Dogs" single.

opposite bottom right: Guffawing during a *Vogue* magazine photo shoot, July 1969.

opposite top: The first double-page spread of the album booklet. The left-hand page illustrates the loneliness and longing of the song "Christmas," while the right-hand page uses stormy weather as analogy for the cruelty in the song "Cousin Kevin."

opposite bottom: The album booklet's second double-page spread features a selection of stage tricks to go with the song "Acid Queen."

Expanding on the Libretto

Contained within the album is a twelve-page booklet of lyrics containing images that act as "signs" toward the meaning contained in the libretto, and as pictorial symbols for key moments in the story. I hoped that additional meanings could be teased-out of the images and expanded through listening to the music, and by interacting with other listeners as they brought their own thoughts to the images, not unlike the way a poem might be read. The typographic cover of the booklet contains text to the lyrics of seventeen of the album's songs, from "Overture" to "Miracle Cure," with "Amazing Journey" appearing on the cover.

The first double-page spread introduces the song "Christmas" on the left-hand page. The image of a window with curtain being drawn back and candle being lit illustrates the loneliness and longing of Tommy, and the hope expressed by Christmas itself. The candle is also a symbol of the light of a single soul penetrating meaningless darkness. A candle lit in the window is a familiar trope representing hope and guide to help someone home. The image on the right-hand page deals with the subject of cruelty and bullying, as contained in the song "Cousin Kevin." It uses weather as a simile for the climate of fear or atmosphere of dread associated with the presence of a monstrous figure. The formal design of storm clouds and lightning are suggestive of routine and patterned behavior.

The second double-page spread, for "The Acid Queen," uses sleight of hand and stage tricks to illustrate visual illusion. The staged magic is used to reference the manipulation of Tommy's mind through drug-induced illusion. The use here of a photograph—generally considered an objective record of fact—further reinforces the notion of trickery in the posed moment. The set was constructed to deliberately reveal small deceptions, such as string holding things in space. Unfortunately, before Photoshop, everything had to be physically in place for the photographer, Barrie Mellor, to capture the completed tableau vivant. The support string was not visible enough—something that was not apparent until we received the final five-by-four-inch transparencies.

Karen Townshend designed and made the uniforms of the tricksters. The man juggling nine balls on the right of the door is Stanley Mouse, a famous psychedelic poster artist from San Francisco who drew the skeleton/roses artwork for the group Grateful Dead. Mouse was living in London at the time, while working at *Nova* magazine and hanging out at The Beatles' Apple headquarters, where he witnessed their final concert on the roof of the building. I mentioned the shoot when he visited my studio at Willoughby House, and he agreed to take part in the photo tableaux. When preparing ideas for the shoot, I was informed that it was physically impossible to juggle more than seven balls, which is why Mouse is shown juggling with nine, although now I understand the record for ball juggling is eleven.

The spread for "Pinball Wizard" was the very last image produced for the album. There was very little time to make the measured, precise, and slow painting required for the artwork. Given the time available, I thought it a good idea to spend a day at a games arcade in Soho and create a photo essay on pinball machines and players with photographer Barrie Meller. We would then be free to select either an appropriate single image or a sequence of images from the series of full-color 35mm transparencies taken on site.

And Tommy doesn't know what day it is

To stand in the rain and catch cold so you die?

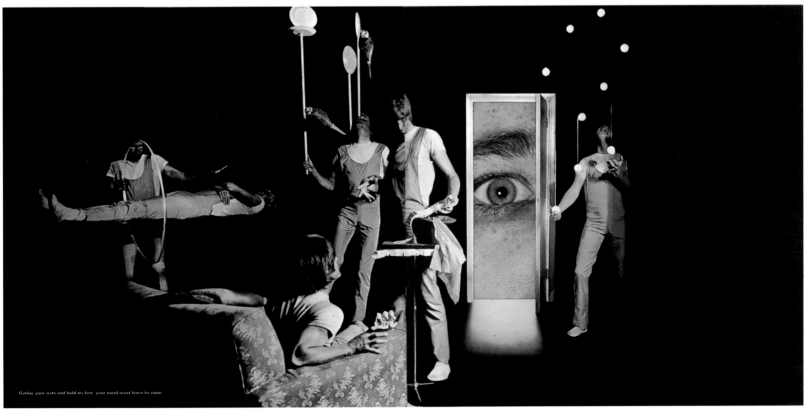

Gather your wits and hold on fast, your mind must learn to roam

But I ain't seen anything like him in any amusement hall . . . That deaf dumb and blind kid sure plays mean pinball!

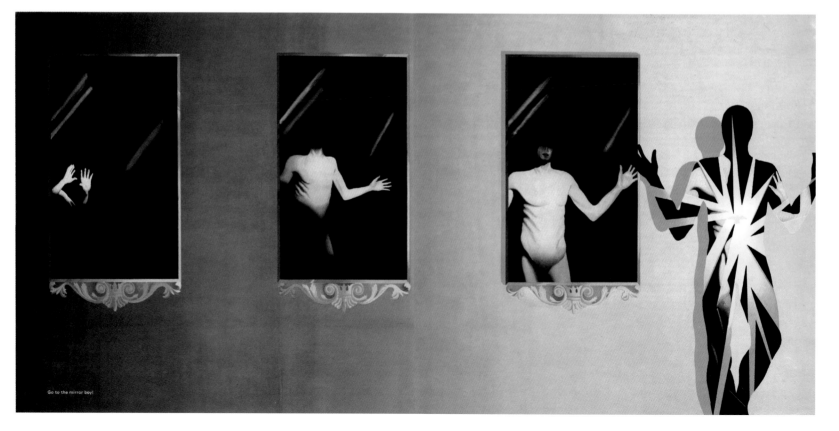

Go to the mirror boy!

opposite top: The third double-spread illustrates "Pinball Wizard" and features a last-minute image photographed on an expedition to a games arcade in Soho, London.

opposite bottom: The song "Go to the Mirror" is illustrated as a continuous sequence in the fourth double-page spread, suggesting the passage of time and coming into being.

❝ Before The Who got big, I wanted them to get bigger and bigger and bigger and bigger until a #1 record and then wrap dynamite around their heads and blow themselves up on TV. Well-presented destruction is what I call a joy to watch."

Pete Townshend to the *International Times*, February 13, 1967

The space-age boy and girl graphic on the pinball machine captured something of the "out of this world" zeitgeist of the time, so I chose it for the spread.

The image for the song "Go to the Mirror" appears next as a continuous sequence across both sides of the fourth spread. It suggests a passage of time—a coming into being, from darkness into light; a moment of self-revelation accounting for a mind in a world otherwise composed of matter, that does not passively mirror reality but actively creates a truth from it. Awakened senses released from deprivation and spiritual isolation. A shattering and at the same time restored feeling of being nowhere and everywhere, nothing and everything at one and the same moment in time.

The fifth spread features the song "Sally Simpson" on its left-hand page. The image questions the nature of the audience for *Tommy* at this stage in the libretto. It is a meditation on the audience and its relationship to the performer. There is something controlling and manipulative in the formal pattern of the audience and the visual rhythm of the pictorial maxim "see no evil, hear no evil, speak no evil" of the three wise monkeys. The cynical conclusion described in the picture is that the crowd is no longer an audience of individual active participants but a collective of acolytes in a trance.

Pete's relationship with his audience was important, and would provide a necessary ingredient to the ambitious narratives of larger projects like *Tommy*, *Lifehouse*, and *Quadrophenia*. *Tommy* may start out as an exploration of the performer/audience relationship but it expands to explore ideas of the master/disciple relationship, wherein understandings may be achieved creating bonds that absorb and

assimilate concepts at a higher level—or it may be an attachment that simply crashes under the weight of expectations.

In the February 13–26, 1967, issue of the *International Times*, Barry Miles asked Pete about auto-destruction as a creative act requiring an audience. "When you've got an audience there it is one of the most exhilarating experiences you can have," Pete replied. "It's THE exhibitionist's delight, to do something really big in front of people . . . I think everyone is a member of an audience; everyone wants to sit back and watch. I do."

Opposite "Sally Simpson," on the right-hand page of the fifth spread, is an artwork to accompany the song "Welcome." According to Pete, the song references the institution of the church and the need for followers to hand over responsibility for their spiritual life as they try to define a way to follow and believe in what by now has become an organization. "Welcome . . . come to my house" accompanies an image of utopian modernist architecture, the type of building constructed in the early part of the twentieth century to encourage healthy living. Creating a cheerful and bucolic environment full of light and fresh air was considered a way to improve the life of those given the opportunity to use it.

Whereas the previous page depicts the Tommy Holiday Camp as a dream, the image on the back cover shows an illusion in ruin to illustrate the song "We're Not Gonna Take It." The image is a reflection on the ossifying and stagnating effect of institutionalized faith—the Holiday Camp as an organization where the audience, attracted to Tommy's new found awareness, thoughtlessly repeat choreographed patterns of instruction, stripping any possible

enlightening experience of its meaning. The song's chorus, "We're Not Gonna Take It," illustrates the rejection of Tommy as spiritual guide just at the moment that his spiritual journey intensifies in the vision of his own unique master/disciple relationship with God.

Perspective, Movement, and Light

By the time I created the artwork for *Tommy*, I had moved away from LSD-inspired forms and returned to the concepts of perception and illusion in which I had held an interest since college. I explored modes of expression through drawing that relied on the careful crafting of graduated tones to render three-dimensional forms on two-dimensional surfaces; drawing that depicted the way things are perceived using visual tropes such as linear perspective to describe pictorial space and chiaroscuro (light and dark shading) as part of the detailed description of surfaces.

The diamond mesh pattern of the globe was not measured but drawn by eye, using guesswork to establish a plausible geometric object with a convincing surface perspective turning rapidly toward its horizon. It took many attempts to create the interlaced structural pattern using tracing paper, transparent enough to see through, to retrace previously drawn crisscross perspective lines as I attempted to correct the perspective of the sloping surface in a way that looked satisfactory, convincing the eye that the surface was in fact turning away, toward the edge of the sphere. Because it is not a measured drawing, the diamond mesh appears to have a right-leaning bias, which might be related to the fact that I am right-handed.

I used gouache to paint the images, a water-based medium consisting of natural pigment, water, and a binding agent (usually gum arabic, also known as acacia gum). It is a perfect opaque medium for creating flat even surfaces of color, though the pigment is known to be "fugitive" in that it is prone to fading in sunlight. When Pete bought some gouache works at my Whitechapel Art Gallery exhibition in 1975, I mentioned, while hanging pictures, that the blue used for the sky on *Tommy* artwork was particularly "fugitive." He enjoyed the use of the word and the thought of sky blue hiding from the sun.

All of the artwork for *Tommy* was carefully painted over a period of ten weeks or more, using a meticulous process of short brush strokes to create careful handcrafted gradations of tone from light to dark. Effects that were previously created by the blending of inks in my psychedelic posters now required hand-painted blends for the four-color separations required to produce original full-color artwork.

Forms would be drawn and cut with a scalpel knife via masks for the larger areas of continuous tone on the outer and inner cover. Tonal gradation was applied using mechanical tools such as the DeVilbiss Airbrush, a slender handheld pen with a nozzle that could supply a fine spray of paint at regular pressure with a delicate trigger to deliver a fine line or cover a large area as required. The pen was supplied with air by a pump that created regular pressure to enable a smooth, continuous spray. These smooth tones and even surfaces reveal a world of objects through a thin veneer of light. This painting process produced still, calm surface illumination. The subjects within the frame of each picture face the viewer directly, and this "frontality" presents a narrow pictorial volume through eye-level compositions, expressing an idea of the shallow living space we all inhabit.

The theme of the sermon was come unto me, love will find a way

A Pop/Classical Fusion

Everyone involved in *Tommy* knew how important it was for the future of The Who. As it progressed, the feeling grew that something special was happening. Pete carried the burden of providing the inspiration and songs for the opera with much support from all those involved, especially Kit Lambert, the group's manager. He kept a very watchful eye on things as they progressed. Lambert was very excited by the whole project. He held bohemian ideas about the artists who worked for him—romantic ideas possibly influenced by his father's work as the composer of English music inspired by traditional British folk songs.

Lambert's artistic vision drove the belief that *Tommy* was an important pop/classical fusion. As the project progressed, the idea of a synthesis between popular culture and high art inspired Lambert to publish the first fifty-thousand-copy print run of the album as a limited edition—a numbered run of fine art prints usually sold in art galleries. The gesture was more about the creative rather than monetary value of the project. During the *Tommy* recording sessions, Lambert also wrote a film script, which he titled *Tommy, 1914–84*. After the album was released, he asked me to create some key visuals to form part of his script presentation to potential backers. I proceeded to produce a series of key visuals as tonal paintings, unaware then that Kit's film version had not been authorized by the band and would lead to significant differences between him and The Who that would never really mend.

I was delighted by just how relaxed the band and Kit were at the idea of a symbolic cover. There was never any doubt that the cover could work without featuring images of the band. My work

on it proceeded and was completed on this assumption, until a production meeting held in the offices of Track Records with Kit, Chris, and representatives from Decca. The Decca people, looking like CIA operatives, had flown in from America to talk about the need for images of the band to be on the album cover for the US market. It was a real blow to the project, and one that came as such a surprise, since there had been no prior indication of a problem.

I panicked. Here was a completed piece of artwork; how would it be possible to insert images of four people onto the existing cover design? The only neutral spaces available in the image were the black diamond shapes, and they were small. I could only think of placing individual headshots in the diamonds, but they risked being on the very edge of legibility. This is not what the label men would have been considering prior to the meeting, but it was the only option that was fully supported back at the Track office.

I needed the band to be doing something relevant to the cover, so I decided they should be reaching out as though touching the surface of the album from inside the image. I managed to arrange a hasty photo shoot with the help once again of Barrie Meller, who borrowed a photographic studio in Bina Gardens, Kensington. Pete and I had a drink and chatted with Barry Fantoni at the Drayton Arms as we waited for the rest of the band to show up.

Once in the studio, we set up a mirror on the floor and had each member of the group lean over into it with arm outstretched while Barry photographed the mirror image. He then supplied me with small black-and-white prints, which I stuck onto the artwork. Immediately there was a problem with symmetry. Four portraits

    There were moments during *Tommy* when I had to clutch the table for support. I felt my stomach contracting and my head spinning. But we wanted more."

Chris Welch on *Tommy*'s launch at Ronnie Scott's, *Melody Maker*, May 3, 1969

would appear very off-center on the cover, so I had to duplicate three of the band members in order to achieve some kind of balance. This created the impression of a seven-piece band on the cover, two pictures each of Keith, Pete, and John, and one of Roger. (The misconception continued when some in the United States felt "TOMMY" was the band's name.)

The Avatar

I have a memory snapshot from back in February 1969, of sitting in Pete's kitchen, showing him the finished artwork for the Tommy cover and trying to find a way of bringing God into the cover copy. The Indian word for God is "Avatar," and, for us, his name was Meher Baba. The cover cast list was where we put him. Somehow, giving God a job description on the album, juxtaposing the ordinary with the extraordinary, seemed appropriate to the project. It was a contrast that wove its way throughout the opera.

The production people at Polydor Records in London produced the first and best printing of the album with the London-based Ernest J. Day and Co. Subsequent printings, especially in America, were very substandard, resulting in poor color on low-quality card and basic paper-engineered packaging.

A very loud and powerful introduction to a huge musical experience was offered at the press launch for *Tommy* within the intimate space of the Ronnie Scott's Jazz Club on Frith Street, London, in May 1969. I like to think that Pete selected Ronnie Scott's after I took him there in the autumn of 1967 to watch the amazing Roland Kirk perform.

Kate and I were driving around Morocco with the sitar-playing artist Vytas Serelis and his wife when the album came out, and on my return things changed. The graphic impact of the cover took me by surprise. Record stores used multiples of the cover to build freestanding displays that would fill the whole window. I heard of customers going into stores to purchase the record, and the package being brought out with great ceremony. I would be at a party and find myself being complimented on creating packaging artwork that held meaning for the music it contained, which would invariably be followed by an enthusiastic analysis of the meaning.

The launch of *Tommy* in May 1969 opened doors to people in the more established media who commissioned some of the most interesting creative work at the time. I began developing a freelance career in illustration, reflecting my growing interests in image making as opinion. There was much to comment on in the variety of cultural and social issues appearing in contemporary journalism. I became the guy to go to for an unusual, lyrical, surreal, dreamlike response to subject matter.

Around the same time, I was commissioned by the *Sunday Times Magazine* to create four artworks for its epic series on the "1,000 Makers of the Twentieth Century," which ran for sixteen weeks during the summer of 1969. Among the other contributors were the painter Ron Kitaj, the photographer David Bailey, the illustrator Robert Grossman, and the cartoonists Ralph Steadman and Gerald Scarfe. I chose to create portraits of the Soviet spy Kim Philby, the existentialist writer Franz Kafka, the German mystic and poet Rainer Maria Rilke, and the expressionist filmmaker Fritz Lang.

the journey of a graphic image
tommy in new forms

Vinyl albums and their twelve-inch cover artworks were physical objects large enough to be a part of people's listening pleasure, and a part of their lives. The graphic image could come to occupy the same space in people's memories as the music itself—the visual equivalent of a tune you can whistle.

As with Maurice Sendak's *Where the Wild Things Are*, the graphic image creates a world of creatures that inform childhood dreams. A moment in time can be forever fixed, as in the Parisian *fin de siècle* lithographic poster "Ambassadeurs: Aristide Bruant" of 1892 by Toulouse-Lautrec, which captures the night life of the city through bold shapes and color in a portrait of the satirical singer Aristide Bruant, or in Saul Bass's poster for the 1955 film noir *The Man with the Golden Arm*, or *Action Comics* #1 from 1938, which featured the first image of Superman on the cover (a pristine copy of which sold for $3.21 million in 2014).

Tommy, too, became a fine art print when it was reprinted in 1992 in a numbered lithograph series. It was part of the "Record Art Collection," a celebration of the twelve-inch vinyl album—a format that had then all but disappeared. It was also used in the scene setting for a rock 'n' roll moment in the film *Almost Famous*, directed by Cameron Crowe in 2000. There, it featured as part of an album collection, providing context and inspiration for the principal character to become a rock journalist.

As live performance in halls and stadiums has grown over the years so has the business of merchandising. For companies such as Live Nation, this has become a global business, using musicians' brand images to merchandise a wide range of products. Over the years, *Tommy* has been licensed to appear on posters, T-shirts, and mugs, among other things, for sale at concerts and through merchandising websites.

In recent years the *Tommy* album cover has been re-appropriated in more unusual ways. In 2011, the Toronto-based company Your Music Memory commissioned me to adapt the artwork for painting onto the front and back of a Gibson SG Special—the type of guitar Pete Townshend used for The Who's 1969 US tour. The guitar was stripped of its controls, pickups, bridge, pegs, and strings and primed with acrylic gesso. I hand-painted the images with acrylic paint and applied a fine background blend with a Chinese made airbrush/compressor.

In 2015, the Italian architect Claudio Catalano wanted to pay tribute to the *Tommy* album and its cover artwork by creating a small work of architecture in the form of a transportable home. The *Nomad Micro House* also doubles as a mobile pavilion. (According to its website, Claudio Catalano Design explores the idea of portable buildings, living pods, and temporary structures using advanced materials and technologies that maximize sustainability and zero impact.)

The cover was also used for a "Bluegrass Opry" version of *Tommy* in 2015. An email request to adapt the original artwork came to me from Louis Meyers, who produced the album for The HillBenders. The adaption was witty and entertaining—a good reason to agree its use.

Around the same time, Jamie Daltrey requested to use the *Tommy* artwork for the branding of a special-edition Roger Daltrey champagne, produced by the Charles Orban vineyard in the Marne Valley, France. A percentage of the proceeds from sales would go to Teen Cancer America. At the Roger Daltrey Cuvée Champagne launch in July 2016, Roger spoke passionately about the British and American charities helping young people through difficult times at a particularly sensitive stage in their lives.

right: A hand-painted Gibson SG Special, created for the Toronto based company Your Music Memory in 2011.

far right top: An interior view of the Nomad Micro House and mobile pavilion, design by the architect Claudio Catalano, 2015.

far right bottom: The *Tommy* album artwork applied to a Rolls-Royce Wraith for a Teenage Cancer Trust charity auction. Visual elements from the cover were stitched and etched to the car's interior surfaces, while the cover artwork was hand-painted onto the hood of the vehicle.

In 2016, the *Tommy* artwork was painted onto the bonnet of a Rolls-Royce Wraith as part of the "Wraith inspired by British Music" campaign. *Tommy* motifs were also stitched and etched on interior surfaces within the Wraith in honor of the music of The Who. Other musicians celebrated included The Kinks, Status Quo, Ronnie Wood, George Martin, and Shirley Bassey. The *Tommy* Wraith was sold at auction as part of the campaign, with the proceeds going to the Teenage Cancer Trust.

Over the years, I have received many requests to use the image, as well as requests to comment on it in articles and academic papers, among other things. Fifty years on, *Tommy* is a graphic image that is still in use, and a graphic story that continues to be told.

My portrait of Philby was published on the magazine's cover on August 24. This was followed by another *Sunday Times Magazine* cover commission to illustrate a survey on readers' dreams. My freelance career was taking off.

The *Tommy* commission highlighted something personal about rock music in the sixties before it became a global business. A loose network of friends would be a part of a band's life, including the manager, who would have a primary interest in what was being made as a proper passport to success. With *Tommy*, it was the manager who supported the ambition of the musicians; it was the author of the opera who commissioned the artist to create its image.

Points of View

On October 5, 1974, the British magazine *Radio Times* published a feature article entitled, "Who Is Tommy?" In it, the journalist Sonya Lopez asked the begetters of *Tommy*—Pete Townshend and Roger Daltrey, novelist and journalist Nik Cohn, and me—how *Tommy* was born.

It seems fairly likely, given his love for a good story, that it would have been Pete's idea for Lopez to also talk with Daltrey, Cohn, and me for her account of the album's creation. The resulting article illustrates his skill at curating the views of others and weaving them into his own creative process. In it, Pete explains how, from his perspective, *Tommy* mixed elements of his own biography with pop-culture references; for Cohn, it was all pinball and the skill of game-playing; for me, it was principally a spiritual journey; for Roger, it was a rock 'n' roll saga, and he *was* Tommy.

Pete spoke about how the use of the senses carried symbolic meaning. "Tommy is deaf, dumb, and blind in the physical plane, the way we are all deaf, dumb, and blind to the spiritual world around us." One of the biggest difficulties he found in creating the film version of *Tommy*—which was in production when the *Radio Times* article appeared—was turning the character into a "real person. Does he carry a white stick, does he bump into doors? The detailing is hard to make decisions on."

Cohn, meanwhile, talked about his love for pinball—"the greatest passion of my life." When he played against Pete and the other members of The Who, however, they all beat him—even Kit Lambert beat him. In the end, he recalled, he had to create "a kind of alter ego, who was Arfur. She was fourteen years old and I promoted her as the greatest pinball artist the world had ever known . . . she proved it by beating Gold Studs Johnny Ace, a rocker from Tottenham. Regrettably, Gold Studs was very dirty in the mouth, so he had to be deaf and dumb. As far as I know, that was the embryo of Tommy."

As I described it to Lopez, the whole thing was a Meher Baba project. "There was a lot of Baba activity in London at the time, and Pete just picked up on it. Baba acted as a catalyst and sparked off the opera."

For Roger, the reality of *Tommy* did not come to him in the recording studio; it came, as it always did, when The Who performed onstage. "For me, it was as though I was just singing Who songs until the second time we played it onstage, and then I realized that I was becoming something else."

Perhaps the truth lies in a combination of all of these viewpoints. As Roger puts it, "Rock 'n' roll is just a mirror of the people you're playing to."

4 the legacy

Chris Charlesworth

the legacy

Tommy wasn't the first rock opera and neither was it the last, but it was the best, the most popular, and the most successful. It has also become the most enduring.

The Who's original double LP, released in May of 1969, spawned an orchestral version, a film with accompanying soundtrack, a slew of theatrical productions, a Broadway musical, scores of live versions in part or whole, cover versions galore, and even a ballet or two. That original LP has been reissued many times over the years in different formats with bonus tracks and is now available as a multi-CD boxed set, with demos, alternate versions, and a high-end booklet—all the bells and whistles the consumer expects in deluxe packages that can cost in excess of $100.

Its legacy for The Who was to give them a stage show that saw them become—if they weren't already—one of the world's great rock bands, a major rock attraction on a par with the Rolling Stones and Led Zeppelin, the only other British groups to contend for title "Greatest Rock Band in the World" during the seventies. With *Tommy* as the centerpiece of their stage show, they became a must-see live attraction, honing a reputation for superlative concert performances that clings to them to this day and ensured their fortunes for the remainder of a discontinuous career that seems everlasting, despite the deaths of Keith Moon in 1978 and of John Entwistle in 2002. It also made the four members of the group and their managers very wealthy—especially Pete Townshend—a natural development of success that bought them fine homes and fancy cars but had its downside in terms of group unity and forward momentum.

Its legacy for the rock industry was to cement the commercial viability of double LPs, to inspire a number of concept albums (many of them ill-advised), and—although *Sgt. Pepper* laid the groundwork—to help make rock acceptable as an art form to vie with painting, literature, classical music, and dance. The Who even performed *Tommy* at staid opera houses in Europe and at the Metropolitan Opera House in New York, thus realizing an important ambition for its producer, Who co-manager Kit Lambert, whose father was a distinguished classical musician.

Having been turned into an orchestral piece, a film, a Broadway show, and a ballet, by the turn of the millennium *Tommy* had entered the pantheon of essential texts for any students of rock history. "The definitive rock opera," is how it is described in the ten-volume *Encyclopedia of Popular Music*, published by the Oxford University Press, the world's most authoritative reference work on rock and pop.

Its legacy for The Who's many fans was to encourage a certain element of "I told you so" when they encountered naysayers in the playground—and, for this writer, already a fan, to tip me over the edge into full-scale indulgence. This led to a career as a music writer, and, as a consequence, a friendship with The Who that saw me work with them in the nineties on the packaging of upgraded CD reissues of their back catalogue. It's probably an exaggeration to state that *Tommy* created a life for me, but it was an important signpost along the way.

The downside for The Who was that it became a millstone around their necks that they have never quite been able to shake off. Realizing this, Townshend and Roger Daltrey, the two surviving members of the group, have now embraced it completely, evidently content with its omnipresence alongside such other rock landmarks as *Sgt. Pepper*, *Dark Side of the Moon*, and *Never Mind the Bollocks*.

It's difficult to pinpoint precisely which member of the group was the first to realize this and become weary of *Tommy*, but the

previous spread: Townshend, Entwistle, and Daltrey take a final bow at London's Wembley Arena, October 1989. The tour, for which they were joined onstage by Simon Philips on drums and eleven other musicians, celebrated the twenty-fifth anniversary of the group's formation and the twentieth anniversary of *Tommy*.

above: The Who performing "The Seeker"—the first post-*Tommy* record they released—on *Top of the Pops*, March 19, 1970.

> I don't think *Tommy* was all about [what] was on the record—I think it's on the stage. The message is much stronger onstage than on record."

John Entwistle to *Crawdaddy!*, December 5, 1971

❞❞ Considered as myth, *Tommy* is intriguing and absurd . . . considered as music, *Tommy* is magnificent, the final crystalization of the hard-rock style in an art as dry, hard, lucid, as unashamedly conventional and finely impersonal as the music of the most severe classicist."

Albert Goldman, *Life*, October 17, 1969

odds-on favorite is John Entwistle, who at one point during 1970— probably when The Who first noticed they were beginning to attract an audience drawn from sycophantic intelligentsia—was heard to mutter in disgust, "Some people think the band's called Tommy and the album's called *The Who*."

While the double album was being mixed and pressed ready for release, The Who rehearsed *Tommy* at Hampstead in North London and Hanwell in the west, and, after the final rehearsal, Pete Townshend and Keith Moon dropped into a nearby pub. "We sat there, both incredulous at how quickly it had come together," Townshend later told Chris Welch of *Melody Maker*. "We noted how suddenly Roger had become something else, and we debated what would happen and how it would change everything."

The Who performed a selection of songs from *Tommy* for the first time at the Casino Club at Bolton in Lancashire on April 22, 1969, and all of the opera's songs they intended featuring in their act three days later at Strathclyde University. It was played again at two further low-key shows in Scotland and one south of the border in Durham, before the press preview at Ronnie Scott's Jazz Club in London's Soho on May 1, the same month the album was released. By all accounts, The Who deafened the assembled writers and guests, among them Marc Bolan of Tyrannosaurus Rex and Ian McLagan of the recently disbanded Small Faces.

"There is a story to the music," said Townshend, after the group had assembled on the cramped stage, banks of speaker cabinets towering around them. "It's the story of Tommy . . . a boy who is born normal, just like you and me. Tommy is born and with the advent of war, his father goes off to fight. Tommy's mother, meanwhile, gets randy and takes a lover. One day, Tommy sees something he shouldn't and is told to keep quiet about it. He witnessed a murder. The shock causes him to go deaf, dumb, and blind."

Some journalists then jokily cried out that this was sick, echoing BBC DJ Tony Blackburn's facile on-air reference to "Pinball Wizard" when it was released as a single in March. "No, it's not sick, ha, ha," continued Townshend. "Contrary to what one hears on Auntie [a snarky nickname for the BBC]. I think Auntie is the sickest thing in this country. . . . The next scene introduces Tommy to Gypsy the Acid Queen, who declares that she will take him into a room for a while and make a man out of a boy. He is later raped by his uncle and gets turned on to LSD. . . . Following this episode, Tommy becomes renowned as a pinball wizard and becomes the hero of the younger generation."

Melody Maker photographer Barrie Wentzell opted not to take any pictures because the room was too small and lighting inadequate. He sat close to the front alongside his *MM* colleague Chris Welch. "We were given seats right next to the stage, right in front of a huge speaker stack," he recalls. "When The Who started up, we were blown backward from the compression and deafened at the sound. My ears were ringing for a week."

In *MM*, Welch wrote, "In the confined space of Ronnie Scott's club, which is more accustomed to the refined rhythms of jazz, the overwhelming intensity of The Who's performance left scores of people literally deaf . . . [but] nobody wanted to miss a minute of the group's riveting rave-up."

Thus began the most illustrious period in The Who's career.

Tommy Goes to America

On May 9, The Who opened the first of two 1969 American tours at the Grande Ballroom in Detroit. Thereafter, accompanied by a skeleton crew, they dragged *Tommy* across America and then Europe, performing it over 160 times until the end of 1970, when they effectively terminated the first phase in the life of their opera. "Assemble the musicians," Townshend was wont to say as the band geared itself for *Thomas*, as he liked to call it. Moon would tap the rim of his snare as the conductor of a symphony orchestra might tap his baton on a music stand. "Stop laughing," he'd yell from behind his drums. "This is serious. It's a fucking opera, ain't it?"

And off they'd go, crashing into the opening chords of the "Overture" and sticking at it, virtually nonstop, until the final verse of "Listening to You," the coda from "We're Not Gonna Take it," an hour and fifteen minutes or so later. It was a marathon performance—something rarely attempted by any rock band before or since—and those fans who caught the opera in its glorious prime were indeed fortunate. Any charges of pretentiousness were deflated by the slightly picaresque sense of humor they displayed when they performed *Tommy* live, much of it emanating from self-deprecating dialogue between Townshend and Moon. They might be playing an opera, but they never forgot it was a rock opera, and that rock was supposed to be fun.

Townshend has recalled that during a *Tommy* performance at the Kinetic Playground, Chicago, on May 29, 1969, the audience—who'd had little opportunity to hear the album and therefore familiarize themselves with the songs—rose at one point and remained standing, evidently entranced by the music and The Who's performance.

"Halfway through, all of a sudden everybody realized that something was working," he told his friend Richard Barnes. "I don't quite know what it was but everybody all at the same time just stood up and stayed standing up. From that moment on they would always stand up at exactly the same point."

By the time *Tommy* reached its climax, no one was ever sitting down. And when the bright lights were switched on during the stirring finish, The Who's auditoria became giant illuminated cathedrals in which, briefly, preachers and congregation were united in a massed celebration of rock music as the force for unification that Pete Townshend truly believed it was meant to be. When the group stepped back and Daltrey intoned, "See me, feel me," over Townshend's softly strummed chords, the crowd hushed, hanging on to every note. And when they fired up again, turbo-charging to the finish as Daltrey sang about how, "listening to you, I get the music," their audiences imagined he was singing not just to them but also about them, and they responded in kind, shouting along, arms waving, fists pumping the air. Huge ovations invariably followed the final sustained chord that climaxed the redemptive saga of Tommy Walker.

The first US *Tommy* tour famously included a show at the Fillmore East in New York on May 16, when the building next door caught fire, prompting a plainclothes police officer to run onstage during The Who's set to advise the audience to evacuate the theater. Daltrey and Townshend, unaware of the officer's identity, pounced on him, and later found themselves in court on assault charges.

The tour closed on June 19 with the last of three nights at the Fillmore West in San Francisco. British *Tommy* gigs in July included a

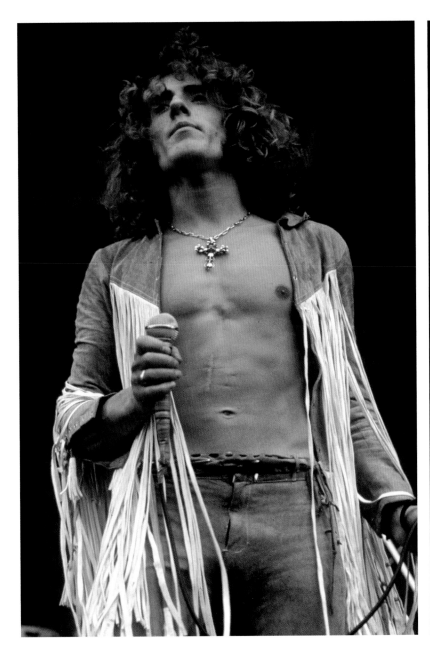

above left: Daltrey onstage at the second Isle of Wight Festival, August 30, 1969, in the fringed outfit he wore for *Tommy* concerts in 1969 and 1970.

above right: A poster for the "Magic Circus" at the Hollywood Palladium, Los Angeles, June 13, 1969, which featured performances by The Who, Poco, and the Bonzo Dog Band, plus "an incredible array of magical, mystical splendors."

pinball wizard of oz
the who and elton john

For the sake of an eye-catching headline, the press—and that includes the British music press—has often exaggerated a rivalry between those who sup at rock's high table. But having played on the same bill as just about everyone somewhere along the line during their long apprenticeship, The Who were friends with pretty much all their rivals.

In the sixties, it was Beatles vs. Stones; in the seventies it was the old guard vs. the punks; and in the nineties it was Oasis vs. Blur. For the most part, this was nonsense. The Beatles were best pals with the Stones, the punks were carping for effect, and even though Liam Gallagher deliberately goaded Damon Albarn with a few lewd comments about his girlfriend, Justine Frischmann, his more mature brother Noel was on good terms with his southern rivals.

On December 22, 1963, as The Detours, The Who supported the Rolling Stones at St. Mary's Hall in Putney, as they did a couple of week later in Forest Hill, London, and as the High Numbers they played with The Beatles in Blackpool on August 16, 1964, with The Kinks also on the bill. All three groups played on the *NME* Poll Winners concert at Wembley Empire Pool on May 1, 1966. In the week preceding this all-star show, on April 26, The Who had appeared at the Links International Club at Boreham Wood near St. Albans in Hertfordshire, where they were supported by an R&B quartet called Bluesology. John Entwistle was later quoted as saying, "I got friendly with their keyboard player, and we were both drowning our sorrows. He was pissed off they wouldn't let him sing, and I was pissed off I wasn't singing enough."

The keyboard player was called Reg Dwight in those days, but by the time he next saw The Who—at Croydon Fairfield Hall on September 21, 1969—he'd changed his name to Elton John. "Saw The Who—excellent," he wrote in his diary when he got back to his home in Pinner.

That night, The Who played *Tommy* in its entirety, and Townshend later rated this show as his favorite ever performance of the opera.

"Oh, Croydon, I could bloody play there all night," he told *ZigZag* magazine in 1974.

Elton wasn't to know it, but the next time he would hear *Tommy* in its entirety, The Who would dedicate it to him. This was at the Roundhouse in London's Chalk Farm on December 20, 1970, when the group headlined a charity benefit show organized by Camden Borough Council to pay for a Christmas Day party for the needy in the borough. Alongside Elton, the support acts included America, Patto, and the local Salvation Army band with a fifty-voice choir who sang a bunch of carols. After dedicating that night's performance of *Tommy* to Elton, for whom he predicted a promising future, Townshend announced that it would be the last time they'd play it onstage. ("Thank Christ for that," Keith Moon shouted in response.) It was the start of a fruitful relationship between the piano-playing songwriter from Pinner and the group formed in nearby Acton.

Elton's next brush with The Who occurred when he was invited to sing "Pinball Wizard" in the *Tommy* movie. Filming took place between May 8 and 10, 1974, at the King's Theatre in Albert Road, Southsea, with fifteen hundred extras on hand to watch, all students from Portsmouth Polytechnic. "In the film, Elton John's performance, for which he wore arguably the tallest platform boots of the glam-rock era, was as bravura a moment as any in his career," writes David Buckley, in his biography of Elton.

Elton's version of "Pinball," which was recorded with his stage group (Davey Johnstone on guitar, Dee Murray on bass, Nigel Olsson on drums, and Ray Thomas on percussion) and produced by Gus Dudgeon at The Who's Ramport Studios in Battersea, reached #7

in the British charts in 1976. "Easily a match for the original," Buckley writes. "The new version came with maniacal triplets on the piano in the intro, trademark E. J. aggressive and trebly acoustic guitar, Ray Cooper's equally wild percussion and Davey Johnstone's pristine rock guitar which interpolated 'I Can't Explain' at the end."

Thereafter the two acts went their own ways, meeting sporadically at industry events until, in 1989, after a seven-year hiatus broken only by Live Aid and an a BPI Awards ceremony, the three original members of The Who undertook a massive tour of the United States, with a few UK dates tacked on the end. In a show of two halves, the first was devoted to *Tommy*. At a benefit show at the Universal Amphitheatre in Los Angeles on August 24—with proceeds going to the Gilbert W. Lindsay Children's Center, United Friends of the Children, The Westside Children's Center, and the Rock and Roll Hall of Fame—an all-star guest lineup took on various roles in the *Tommy* segment of the show, one of only two complete performances of

the rock opera on the tour. For this, Elton John reprised his cinematic role as the Pinball Wizard.

The show easily sold out, with ticket sales totaling $2,050,782 from a crowd of 5,812. In addition, the performance was broadcast live as a pay-per-view television event and recorded for inclusion on a subsequent live album and video.

In 1991, The Who replayed the compliment by recording "Saturday Night's Alright for Fighting" for the album *Two Rooms: Celebrating the Songs of Elton John and Bernie Taupin*, a tribute set that also included contributions from Eric Clapton, the Beach Boys, George Michael, Rod Stewart, Kate Bush, and others. With Pete Townshend's brother-in-law, Jon Astley, on drums, Townshend, Daltrey, and Entwistle made the song their own, seguing neatly into Pete singing "Border Song" halfway through, thus bringing out the contrast between Roger and Pete's voices—a familiar Who trait—and adding a flavor of The Who to their tribute to their friend.

date at the Royal Albert Hall with Chuck Berry, at which trouble broke out among rockers in the audience. This was followed by a short trip back to America to play Tanglewood and the band's now legendary appearance at the Woodstock festival, detailed elsewhere in this book. Then it was back to Britain for the Isle of Wight Festival, a few more UK shows, and the first of their opera house performances.

The shows at European opera houses realized another longstanding ambition for Kit Lambert to put one over on the stuffy classical music establishment. The first, at Amsterdam's Concertgebouw in the Netherlands on September 29, was professionally recorded for a Dutch radio broadcast and subsequently released as a bootleg album—the first from many Who shows in this era, and certainly one of the best. As befitting the occasion, The Who turned in a superb performance. Townshend explained from the stage that The Who had decided to give *Tommy* its opera house premiere in Amsterdam not just because they thought it a great city but also because it was more representative of a European capital than London. On the tapes of the show, the vocals are especially well recorded, as is the guitar and bass, though the drums are on the muddy side. "Overture" emerges as a fine instrumental in its own right, and an appropriate and dramatic prelude to what follows. "Amazing Journey" is wonderfully charged and powerful, with Daltrey especially on fine form. This moves into the instrumental "Sparks," taken at a furious pace, with Entwistle playing some manic bass lines. When they reach the end of *Tommy*—a medley of twenty-one integrated songs, no less, performed virtually back-to-back—it takes them just over twenty seconds to catch their breath before launching into a scorching "Summertime Blues."

Such energy put The Who's dedication to the art of stagecraft into sharp focus. The audience response, perhaps befitting the venue, consists of polite applause rather than overt cheers and whistles. The final number, "My Generation," had been newly reconceived as a fifteen-minute medley, offering a short "history" of The Who in a seamless flow of music from the 1965 single to reprised sections from *Tommy*, followed by several improvised passages, plus snatches of "Pinball Wizard" and the instrumental "The Ox"—the latter prompted by a furious drumroll from Keith Moon and climaxing with screeching guitar solos and crashing riffs.

The two-hour show that The Who presented at this time continued to reach new heights of excitement and excellence wherever they went. They had played so often together by this time—probably more shows than any other rock band of their generation—that they now performed with such cool panache that on their best nights they could take your breath away. Townshend careered and leaped around the stage, his right arm spinning wildly; Daltrey tossed his microphone into the air, then drew it in on its cord like a lasso; Moon turned his massive kit into a lead instrument, juggling his sticks as the group's relentless power spiraled out from his arms and legs; and Entwistle just stood there, nonchalantly underpinning everything, the foundation stone without which it might all collapse. Vocals, guitars, and drums meshed into a seamless whole that no other band has ever been able to emulate. Yet it wasn't a show rehearsed to the point of sterility—it sounded raucous and fresh, and, during this era, The Who turned in performances as good as the one at the Concertgebouw night after night.

above: Moon onstage at the Metropolitan Opera House in New York, June 7, 1970.

opposite top left: *Live at Leeds* was first released in May 1970, with parts of *Tommy*—the "Sparks" instrumental and "See Me, Feel Me"—reprised during an extended "My Generation." Not until the entire Leeds University show became available in 1995 did it include all the *Tommy* played that night, February 14, 1970.

opposite top right: Daltrey, with Emmaretta Marks from the cast of *Hair*, at a party in New York, June, 1970.

A New Decade

Further opera-house performances of *Tommy* took place at the Coliseum in London's Covent Garden, on December 14—another towering performance, this one captured on film—followed by venues in Paris, Copenhagen, Cologne, Hamburg, Berlin, and a second at the Concertgebouw. The Who's final opera-house show was at the Metropolitan Opera House in New York on June 7, 1970, when they played two shows to open another US tour. Although the Met concerts were promoted as being the last ever performances of *Tommy*, this wasn't the case; *Tommy* was performed at all The Who's shows for the remainder of the year. Twenty years later, Roger Daltrey rated the Met concerts as the finest The Who ever played. Ever the devil's advocate, Townshend considered the shows "dire."

"Wow! To watch The Who onstage at any time is an exciting experience, but to watch The Who onstage at the Metropolitan Opera House, through gold chandeliers and Warren Beatty's hair (he was right in front of me, plus Julie Christie, of course), was not merely mind-blowing, it was mind-devastating," wrote Vicki Wickham in *Melody Maker*. "The Who's performance on both shows was superb . . . the most exciting group in the world."

The *Tommy* shows in early 1970 included the legendary concert at Leeds University's Refectory on Valentine's Day, February 14, that was recorded for *Live at Leeds*, long acclaimed as one of the great live albums of this or any other era. The original single-LP edition of *Leeds*, released the following May, did not include *Tommy*, but when it was upgraded in 1995 to include every song The Who played that night, the opera occupied all of the second CD in the package.

There would be another US tour in the summer of 1970; a reprise of *Tommy* at that year's Isle of Wight Festival at the end of August, which was professionally recorded and filmed; and more UK and European dates in the autumn. This all led up to what was billed (again) as the final performance of *Tommy*, at London's Roundhouse on December 20, when they were supported by a bespectacled up-and-coming piano-playing singer and songwriter whose first hit, "Your Song," would enter the charts in a month's time. Before The Who launched into *Tommy* that night, Townshend expressed the view that Elton John had a big future, then promptly dedicated the night's performance of their opera to him.

It wasn't the last performance of *Tommy*, of course—just the end of the first phase of *Tommy*'s lifespan.

Grands Ballets and Rock Steady

Over the next few years, *Tommy*, as played by The Who, would become abridged, with most of its songs discarded. "Welcome," Entwistle's "Cousin Kevin," and the lengthy "Underture" were never played, and "Sally Simpson" generally got the chop, too. By 1971, only "Amazing Journey," "Sparks" (which, with its layered dynamics, sudden octave drops, and multiple rising crescendos, invariably brought audiences to their feet), "Pinball Wizard," and the so-called "See Me, Feel Me" climax remained. In the meantime, however, *Tommy* had taken on a life of its own outside of The Who, sometimes with but often without their support.

The first known cover of a *Tommy* song was recorded by Jennifer Warnes, who, in 1969, and calling herself simply "Jennifer," came

out with a version of "See Me, Feel Me." Heavily orchestrated, it was released only in the US but failed to chart. Warnes, of course, would go on to enjoy a distinguished singing career, most notably collaborating with Leonard Cohen. In 1971, camp keyboard maestro Liberace recorded a live version of the "Overture" from *Tommy*, as released on his *Love and Music Festival* album. Two years later, the folksy British MOR act the New Seekers would record "See Me, Feel Me"—for a double A-side with "Pinball Wizard"—and take it to #16 in the UK charts. Soon, there would be a slew of cover versions on the market, among them a synthesizer-heavy electronic instrumental album of ten *Tommy* songs by Joe Renzetti and Tony Luisa from Philadelphia on Viva Records; a twelve-minute, virtually unidentifiable medley arrangement by jazz drummer Buddy Rich on his 1975 album *Big Band Machine*; and a rather embarrassing late entry by Donny and Marie Osmond, who performed "Pinball" and "See Me, Feel Me" on *The Donny and Marie Show* in 1977. In the fullness of time, there would be a ska version called *Tommy: A Rock Steady Opera* by a band called Ye Olde English; a remarkably adept tribute version by New Jersey group The Smithereens, who stripped *Tommy* down to just over forty minutes by recording only what they considered to be its highlights; and, perhaps inevitably, a classical adaptation for viola, cello, and two violins by the Vitamin String Quartet from Los Angeles.

In the meantime, and more ambitious, was a *Tommy* ballet, arranged and choreographed by Les Grands Ballets Canadiens and staged in 1971–1972. The performers danced to The Who's album played at volume through a state-of-the-art stereo system. "It was

one of the first shows I saw with large backdrops on which black-and-white pictures of the band and close-ups were displayed and then changed," reports Ed Hanel, the noted Who archivist and discographer. "The sound system was fantastic." This, the first of several dance-based interpretations of *Tommy*, arrived in New York in 1971, and it also played at the Théâtre des Champs-Élysées in Paris. Also in 1971 came an orchestral adaptation by the Seattle Opera at the city's Moore Theatre, with a then largely unknown Bette Midler taking on two roles, as the Acid Queen and Tommy's mother. According to the *Houston Post*, it was "literally stunning in its totally original artistic conception."

"She has to do with the ferociousness of female sexuality," Midler told the *Post* of her role as the Acid Queen. "It's not just a sexual seduction. It's symbolic of the gigantic commercialization of femaleness." Warming to her theme, Bette—never one to mince her words—added, "Its message is timeless. It's about how we cover our eyes, our ears and cut off our tongues and how we isolate ourselves and how we are isolated by society. The real message, I guess, is how important it is to find freedom and that you can't find it through God or drugs or through anything but yourself. *Tommy* will open up something people are not ready for."

A second theatrical production of *Tommy* was staged in March of 1972 at the Aquarius Theatre in Los Angeles under the direction of Joel Rosenweig, whose student production of the rock opera was his college thesis. Having evidently obtained Townshend's approval, his show was given a lukewarm review by *Billboard*, the American music industry's trade paper.

top left: The pinball motif on the cover of Lou Reizner's orchestral production of *Tommy*.

bottom left: *Tommy* interpreted as a ballet in Paris in 1971.

above right: US record producer Lou Reizner, who died in 1977, was best known for his work with Rod Stewart until he took on the *Tommy* orchestral project.

dark sides and futures passed
a brief history of concept albums

Tommy helped persuade those who controlled the purse strings at record companies that there was money to made by being a bit less conservative and giving artists a looser rein.

There is a grey area that separates rock operas from concept albums or even musicals that feature rock music. *Tommy* certainly wasn't an inspiration for the work of Andrew Lloyd Webber and Tim Rice, nor was it for albums like Jethro Tull's *Thick as a Brick* (supposedly a collection of songs that spoof the kind of stories found in local newspapers), Elton John's *Captain Fantastic and the Brown Dirt Cowboy* (an autobiography in song about the travails of Elton and his co-songwriter Bernie Taupin before they became famous), or Jeff Wayne's *War of the Worlds* (which is based on the science-fiction book by H. G. Wells).

These examples from the seventies are related only insofar as they all contain songs that are in some way interconnected; that those who produced them intended these LPs to be more than just another collection of random songs. In this respect, *Tommy* did serve to demonstrate to the music industry that lengthy rock works of a more cerebral nature could become commercially successful. It is all too easy to imagine an earnest young musician attempting to explain his conceptual idea to an A&R man who rolls his eyes upward and responds with, "How about another album of sexy rock with two or three hit singles instead?"

The Moody Blues' *Days of Future Passed*, often cited as the first "progressive rock" LP, was recorded in 1967 and tells a vague story about a day in the life of a Mr. Ordinary. In August of the same year, Keith West reached #2 in the UK with "Excerpt from a 'Teenage Opera,'" an ambitious song about someone called Grocer Jack. "The 'opera' was never completed," says guitarist Steve Howe, who played on the track. "As the single cost so much, EMI shrunk the budget, so

[producer] Mark Wirtz wasn't able to continue with the same level of extravagance throughout the intended album."

More closely related to *Tommy* was the Pretty Things' *S. F. Sorrow*, based on a narrative by singer Phil May about the life of the title character, released in December 1968. Sebastian F. Sorrow's story is told in the liner notes on the LP, but it failed to make any impression on the LP charts.

An act closer in spirit to The Who that around this time devoted time to concept records was The Kinks. There was an element of rivalry between the two groups, with The Kinks representing North London and The Who the West. Both were led by outstanding songwriters and had endured volatile episodes that could have fragmented lesser acts. Before The Who even began work on *Tommy*, The Kinks were recording an album with the unwieldy title *The Kinks Are the Village Green Preservation Society*, for which Ray Davies wrote a series of songs that were loosely connected in that they seemed to mourn the passing of English traditions. Subsequent *Preservation* albums by The Kinks used the village green as a metaphor for the way in which property developers run roughshod in their zeal to demolish and build anew, not always with beneficial results. The album, which contained no hit singles, was a flop by Kinks standards; although it was released just six months before *Tommy*, no one drew any parallels between the two.

A year later, The Kinks released another concept LP, *Arthur (or the Decline and Fall of the British Empire)*, which, like *Village Green*, attracted positive reviews but failed to sell well. In perhaps striving to explain why, Kinks biographer Johnny Rogan later observed that,

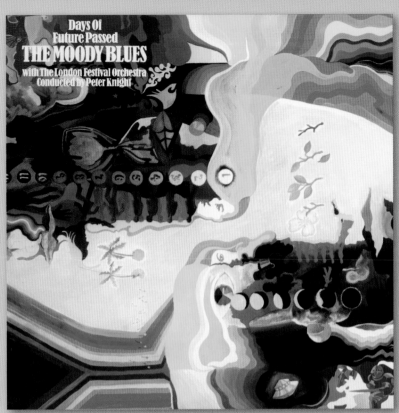

top left: The Moody Blues' *Days of Future Passed* (1967), widely considered to be the first progressive-rock album.

top right: The Pretty Things' *S.F. Sorrow* (1968), which predated The Who's own rock opera by five months.

bottom right: The Kinks' *The Kinks Are the Village Green Preservation Society* (1968), the final album by the original quartet of Ray Davies, Dave Davies, Pete Quaife, and Mick Avory.

"[Ray] Davies's celebration of the mundane was far removed from the studious iconoclasm of *Tommy* and its successors."

None of this dampened enthusiasm for concept albums by the upper tier of British rock. Yes released *Tales from Topographic Oceans* in late 1973, a double LP that singer Jon Anderson claimed loftily was "loosely based on a footnote in Paramahansa Yogananda's 1946 philosophical tome *Autobiography of a Yogi*," while Genesis joined the fray in 1974 with *The Lamb Lies Down on Broadway*. Largely the work of singer Peter Gabriel, it tells the story of Rael, a Puerto Rican youth living in New York City whose journey of self-discovery involves many curious incidents and characters. Both of these albums were double LPs, and on release both groups delivered them in their entirety to audiences that remained largely indifferent. No doubt they'd have preferred to hear music with which they were already familiar.

When The Who did the same thing, however, the energy they transmitted gave *Tommy* an extra dimension. Regrettably, the same didn't happen with *Quadrophenia*, their second rock opera, released in 1973. Another double LP, *Quadrophenia* was virtually a Townshend solo project for which the other members of The Who acted as his session musicians. More advanced musically than *Tommy*, it is harder to assimilate yet ultimately just as rewarding, not least because it references The Who's own history, and it is clear from the number of reissues and revivals that Townshend rates it just as highly as *Tommy*.

Unfortunately, there were problems performing *Quadrophenia* live. At its best, The Who was a free-flowing, high-energy machine, capable of improvising at will and flying off at remarkable tangents—usually on the spur of the moment, at Pete Townshend's whim. The backing tapes of synthesizer music that were necessary to present *Quadrophenia* authentically onstage dictated a different approach, a more rigid style that allowed little room for The Who to play together in the manner in which they excelled. When the tapes malfunctioned, it threw everyone off balance, and *Quadrophenia* came crashing down, reducing Townshend to a spluttering rage. The other three, eager to please but concerned their composer occasionally aimed too high, grew equally frustrated. So, too, did the fans. Eventually, rather like *Tommy*, *Quadrophenia* was edited down, and only a few songs survived as live pieces. Released to coincide with The Who's first UK and US tours for two years, it reached #2 in both countries' album charts.

Perhaps closer to *Tommy* was Pink Floyd's *The Wall* (1979), in which the latter group's bass player and leader Roger Waters railed against all manner of establishment figures that got his goat, from schoolmasters to politicians, all seen through the feeling of isolation he felt onstage. He decoded the barrier between band and audience as the barriers that exist between people at large—a weighty philosophical concept that many failed to grasp. Pink Floyd attempted to explain this with spectacular concerts in which a giant wall was erected between them and their audience as they played; when, like The Who, they eventually regrouped, the eternally discontented Waters was not among them.

All of this occurred a decade after The Who took *Tommy* on the road, and when staging of rock had become far more sophisticated, much of which could be put down to the efforts of the Floyd themselves. Nevertheless, *Tommy* has outdistanced them all, be they the efforts of the Moody Blues, Pretty Things, Kinks, Yes, Genesis, Pink Floyd, and whoever else you care to name.

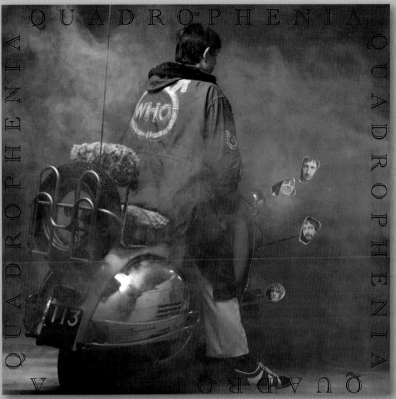

top left: Yes's *Tales from Topographic Oceans* (1973), a concept album based on Paramahansa Yogananda's *Autobiography of a Yogi*.

top right: The Who's *Quadrophenia* (1973).

bottom right: Pink Floyd performing *The Wall* at Earls Court, London, June 16, 1980.

To get all those people there was the event. Just like Woodstock could be criticized for all its problems, it started the festivals. And this, too, was a first."

Lou Reizer on the Rainbow Theatre shows to *Rolling Stone*, January 18, 1973

"The hellfire sincerity of its music is enough to make it a more relevant entertainment than *Hair*," wrote Nat Freedland. "But theatrically the show handles its explosive material rather too timidly."

A much higher profile was accorded to US producer Lou Reizner's orchestral production with the London Symphony Orchestra and Chamber Choir, first as a double LP and then as a concert at London's Rainbow Theatre. Reizner, who had made his name as the producer of Rod Stewart's first two solo albums—both outstanding blends of original material and tasteful interpretations—somehow got Townshend and The Who onside when he turned his attention to *Tommy*. Daltrey took the role of Tommy, Entwistle was Cousin Kevin, and Townshend sang those parts attributed to the narrator. The guest stars included Ringo Starr, Rod Stewart, Sandy Denny, Maggie Bell, Steve Winwood, Richie Havens, and the actor Richard Harris.

Packaged in an opulent hard slipcase with a double pinball motif, and including a twenty-eight-page booklet with paintings of the guest stars in costumes appropriate to the roles they sang, the album was released in November 1972, accompanied by a big PR campaign. On December 9, there were two orchestral performances at the Rainbow, with most of those who sang on the album present, though Peter Sellers played the part of the Doctor, as Richard Harris was unavailable, and Keith Moon deputized for Ringo as Uncle Ernie—a role in which he excelled, at least according to *New Musical Express*, for which Roy Carr noted, "As a fiddling pervert he was the epitome of warped depravity, to the extent that you could almost smell him."

The two concerts were originally planned for the Royal Albert Hall, but when the hall's authorities realized the LSO and choir was going to perform The Who's *Tommy*, permission was refused. "The manager of the Albert Hall told me he considered *Tommy* to be unsavory," Reizner told the press. The ban may have had something to do with the trouble that broke out at the RAH during the Who shows there in July 1969, following which there was a general ban on rock at the venue.

The two concerts at the Rainbow were a great success, both sellouts, and over £15,000 was raised for the Stars Organisation for Spastics. "Demand for the tickets has been tremendous," said Rosemary James, who ran the Rainbow's box office. "We thought the demand for tickets for the Osmonds was chaotic, but this beats all." Townshend, overwrought through working on *Quadrophenia*, The Who's next big project, was too exhausted to enjoy the evening. "[It] should have been a wonderful evening, [but it] became an excuse to celebrate, and to drink, and thus to fuck things up," he writes in *Who I Am*.

There was a second "Lou Reizner's *Tommy*" production in Australia in March 1973, which gained some legitimacy when Moon—on a roll as Uncle Ernie—accepted an invitation to join the cast in Melbourne and Sydney, the only member of The Who to do so. Finally, yet another run at the Rainbow on December 13 and 14 that year featured a different cast—among them David Essex, Elkie Brooks, Vivian Stanshall, Roy Wood, and Jon "Dr. Who" Pertwee—after which this version of *Tommy* seems to have been laid to rest.

It was notable that Kit Lambert—much to his chagrin, in view of his background in classical music—was never involved in Reizner's

top left: Moon as Uncle Ernie during the orchestral *Tommy* concert at London's Rainbow Theatre, December 9, 1972. In a letter to *Dear Boy* author Tony Fletcher, Patti Salter, Moon's girlfriend at the time, described how Moon tried to buy a seedy-looking raincoat to wear in the film: "After purchasing the baggiest one he could find we then drove around London in the Rolls looking for puddles. When we found a nice big dirty looking one he stepped out of the car, and just lay down and rolled around in it. People stared and couldn't believe their eyes."

top right: The cast at the orchestral *Tommy* concert. Daltrey is stage center, with Townshend, Entwistle, and Moon on the right.

bottom right: Maggie Bell, Roger Daltrey, Richie Havens, and Lou Reizner during rehearsals at the Rainbow.

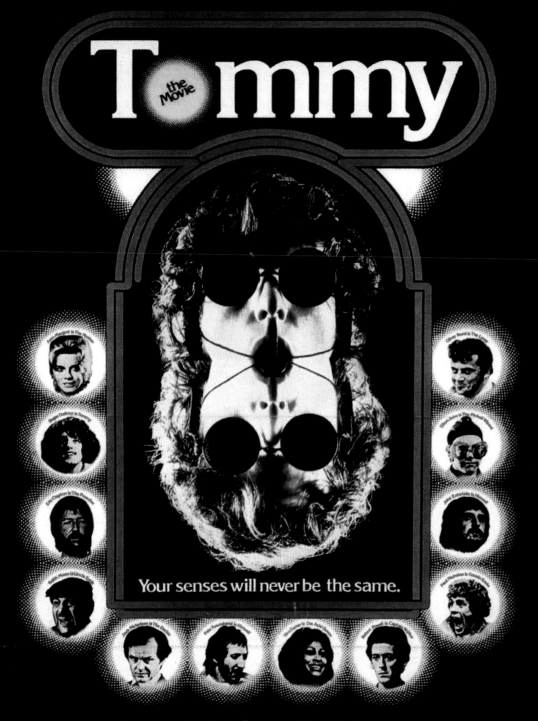

left: "Your senses will never be the same":
a poster for the all-star *Tommy* movie.

orchestral production of *Tommy*, either on record or onstage. This oversight—which is how Townshend has described it—would be exacerbated by Lambert's exclusion from the next *Tommy*-related venture, a project that in scope and ambition dwarfed all that had come before.

From Stage to Screen

Back in 1967, when Pete Townshend was musing over a poem he'd written called "The Amazing Journey," any suggestion that his pet project might one day become a movie with a budget of five million dollars, directed by Ken Russell and starring Ann-Margret, Oliver Reed, and Jack Nicholson, would have seemed as ridiculous to him as some of Keith's Moon's wilder antics after downing a second bottle of Courvoisier.

Film production had always been high on The Who's agenda. Managers Kit Lambert and Chris Stamp were both working in the film industry when Lambert chanced on The Who, then billed as the High Numbers, at the Railway Hotel in Harrow one night in July 1964. He was looking for a group to appear in a film about a youthful hullabaloo that he and Stamp wanted to make, but this was soon forgotten when they decided instead to become the group's managers. In the event, the pair did film The Who at the Railway in August that year, resulting in the first ever footage of the group, and their enthusiasm for film didn't waver as The Who's career developed during the sixties. As a result, there is probably more early footage of The Who performing live than of any of their peers, much of which is today available on DVD and online.[8]

The film rights to *Tommy* were optioned by MCA/Universal, the parent company of Decca Records, The Who's American label, not long after the release of the original album, but for a while the group, and Townshend in particular, wanted to forge ahead without looking backward. In 1971, they concentrated on *Who's Next*, an album developed from another, somewhat impenetrable Townshend concept called *Lifehouse*, and in 1973 they came up with *Quadrophenia*, a double album similar to *Tommy* only insofar as it told a story that climaxed in redemption, this time about an alienated mod called Jimmy.

During the *Quadrophenia* sessions, proposals for filming *Tommy* were back on the table. By now, The Who's managerial situation was in flux, due in part to Lambert and Stamp's dereliction of duties and the emergence of potential successors in Bill Curbishley, who operated in London, and Peter Rudge, whose New York office looked after The Who's US affairs.[9] Meanwhile, the impresario Robert Stigwood, an early ally of The Who and the manager of Eric Clapton and the Bee Gees, had come forward as a possible producer of a *Tommy* film. Stigwood had produced a successful screen adaptation of the Andrew Lloyd Webber and Tim Rice musical *Jesus Christ Superstar*, and with his track record was better placed than anyone else in The Who's circle to take the project forward. Which is precisely what he did, securing a budget from Columbia Pictures of five million dollars and signing up Ken Russell, The Who, and various others. Daltrey would play Tommy, Ann-Margret his mother, Oliver Reed his mother's lover, Tina Turner the Acid Queen, Elton John the Pinball Wizard, Eric Clapton the Preacher, Jack Nicholson the Doctor,

opposite top: Elton John in his outsize boots, fronted by Entwistle, Daltrey, and Townshend, in the *Tommy* film's "Pinball Wizard" sequence.

opposite bottom: Tina Turner as the Acid Queen. In 1975, Turner released an album entitled *Acid Queen* that contained a cover of The Who's "I Can See for Miles."

right: Oliver Reed as "Uncle" Frank Hobbs—the name assigned to Tommy's mother's lover in the movie.

Entwistle Cousin Kevin, and, inevitably, Moon would play Uncle Ernie. As on the Lou Reizner project, Townshend acted as a narrator.

Production began in the spring of 1974 on locations in and around Portsmouth, with the opening and closing outdoor scenes shot in the Lake District in the northwest of England. Elton John's endearing "Pinball Wizard" sequence was filmed at a theater in Southsea; it was reported that he agreed to take part only if he was allowed to record the song with his own band and keep the enormous platform-heeled boots he was given to wear.[10] Somewhere along the line a decision was made that the film would contain no dialogue, with all parts sung like a grand opera. Unfortunately, not everyone could sing, so Oliver Reed and Jack Nicholson were obliged to warble their songs as well as they could, which wasn't very well at all. Still, Ann-Margret was eye-catching, and she made a fine mother; the scene in which she cavorts amid foam, baked beans, and liquid chocolate spewing from a TV set was judged to be the film's highlight.

Quite what all this had to do with Townshend's original conception of *Tommy* is anyone's guess, but Ken Russell had a reputation for over-the-top sequences in the films he directed, so the scene blended in perfectly with other garish extravagances he laid on. In fact, that scene called for a new song, "Champagne"—one of four additional songs that Townshend wrote for the movie. Other liberties taken with the storyline include the murder of Tommy's father by his mother's lover (as opposed to the other way around), which ensured that Oliver Reed's character was the villain of the piece, a role he assumed with gusto; the updating of the whole story to the seventies, which was more in keeping with Russell's interpretation

of the narrative; and the razing of Tommy's Holiday Camp by his followers, who also do off with Tommy's mother and her lover, evidently in revenge for commercializing the whole enterprise and inflicting deafness, dumbness, and blindness on them all.

Feelings about the film among Who fans were mixed, not least because many felt that Russell had in some way trivialized Townshend's *Tommy*, turning it into something that was part comedy, part camp, and part burlesque, and—perhaps most damning—something other than rock music. Nevertheless, all agreed it was a triumph for Daltrey. "Roger is somewhat of a natural performer and has a good sense of cinema," Russell told David Litchfield, in an interview that originally appeared in *The Image.* "He didn't know anything of the technique but suggested some good cinematic ideas, good ideas six tenths of the time which is exceptional."

The film, along with the soundtrack, was released in March 1975 and was an instant box-office success. Ann-Margret received a Golden Globe Award and was nominated for an Oscar in the "Best Actress" category. Townshend was nominated for an Oscar for his work on the music, the film as a whole was nominated for "Best Picture (Musical or Comedy)," and Daltrey was nominated in the "Most Promising Newcomer" category.

Most reviews were positive. The *New York Times* reviewer wrote, "Russell's *Tommy* virtually explodes with excitement on the screen. A lot of it is not quite the profound social commentary it pretends to be, but that's beside the point of the fun. *Tommy* . . . is mad, funny, irreverent, passionately overproduced, very, very loud and

the wild man
introducing ken russell

Overweight, florid, and with a mop of hair that was impervious to the attentions of a comb, Ken Russell was as controversial as he was flamboyant, and he threw himself into directing the *Tommy* film with all the enthusiasm that Keith Moon put into playing his drums.

"This country's in a weird, feeble, grotesque state, and it's about time it got out of it," Russell, effusive as ever, explained to the host of LWT's *Russell Harty Show*, on March 27, 1975. "And the reason it could get out of it is rock music, and I think that Townshend, The Who, Roger Daltrey, Entwistle, Moon, could rise this country out of its decadent, ambient state more than Wilson and those crappy people could ever hope to achieve."

With a slew of provocative films behind him, many of them featuring nudity and blasphemy, Russell was the obvious choice to transfer the story of the deaf, dumb, and blind boy to the silver screen. Inspired by classical music from early in his career, he'd worked on documentaries of Prokofiev, Elgar, Bartok, Debussy, Delius, and Richard Strauss for the BBC art show *Monitor*, so the leap into rock opera seemed like a natural progression.

Perhaps more importantly, Russell was noted for excess in films like *Women in Love* (1969), now widely regarded as the best film he directed. The movie, which features a nude wrestling scene that shows glimpses of male genitalia, stars Glenda Jackson, who won an Oscar for "Best Actress," and Oliver Reed, with whom Russell worked often and subsequently proposed for the role of Tommy's father. It also earned Russell an Oscar nomination for "Best Director." Equally provocative was *The Devils* (1971), also starring Reed, this time opposite Vanessa Redgrave, which features scenes involving nuns masturbating with crucifixes, and which as a result was either banned or heavily censored. (It wasn't until 2006 that an uncut version of the film was finally shown, albeit only at film festivals.)

It was fellow director and music critic Tony Palmer who brought *Tommy* to Russell's attention when they were working together at the BBC in the early seventies. "I liked the music but couldn't make any sense of the story," Russell told *The Image*. "I got Pete [Townshend] to give me every piece of literature he had about it and I read through a pile a mile high. I pointed out that there would need to be more songs to clarify the story. It never occurred to me to use dialogue."

But Russell also identified with the spiritual side of *Tommy*, telling Litchfield, "Before I started writing the screenplay I appreciated exactly what it was to [Townshend] and that it was a spiritual piece. I didn't want to impose my own ideas so I asked him precisely what he meant by each piece. I believe that people don't know why they do things [and] I think that an instinctive artist like Pete Townshend doesn't necessarily have to explain why he wrote or what it means exactly. I think the trouble with the twentieth century is that people want to try and explain things too much."

Nevertheless, Russell was obliged to create situations in his film that moved the plot along and, to a degree, explained the storyline more implicitly than Townshend had in his libretto. "I did a very long treatment before I wrote it, and [Townshend] said, 'Yes, that's right.' I think there was only one thing that he disagreed with in that."

Russell may have hit it off with Townshend, but the same cannot be said of his relationship with Keith Moon. In his Moon biography *Dear Boy*, Tony Fletcher reports that the first time Russell met with the group, at their Ramport Studios in Battersea, South London, Moon was six hours late. "In Russell's world, that was sufficient grounds for instant dismissal," writes Fletcher, "and he raged at

right: Russell at work behind the camera in 1975.

Townshend that most directors would not tolerate such timekeeping. Clearly, the discipline of Russell's beloved classical music world ill-prepared him for the informality of rock 'n' roll. But it could well have helped Russell decide, as Oliver Reed recalls, that he 'didn't want Moon to be involved in the film at all.'" When Fletcher approached Russell for anecdotes about Moon for his book, the director responded by stating that everything he had to say about Moon was contained in his autobiography. "He wasn't mentioned once," Fletcher adds.

Though his film of *Tommy* wasn't the unmitigated success he hoped it would be, Russell went on to direct Roger Daltrey again in *Lisztomania* (1975), a biopic of the Hungarian composer Franz Liszt, with a soundtrack composed by classically trained Rick Wakeman, the keyboard player of Yes. In his day, Liszt's piano playing attracted scores of impressionable women to his concerts, which gave rise to the phenomenon that gave the film its title. This presented many

opportunities for the composer to indulge his promiscuous tendencies, so it will come as no surprise that Russell's film concentrates on Liszt's many infidelities and adulterous affairs.

To an extent, Russell softened the excess later in his career, though *The Whore* (1991) speaks for itself, and he was the natural choice to direct the BBC's four-part serialization of *Lady Chatterley* (1993), starring Joely Richardson and Sean Bean, and which, by Russell's standards, was relatively chaste. Later in life, he won many awards and seemed content with the unofficial title of "the wild man in British cinema."

Russell died aged eighty-four on November 27, 2011, and was survived by three of his four wives and eight children. "'Wake 'em up' was generally his watchword, and it was certainly true that you could never go to sleep in a Russell film," the noted film critic Derek Malcolm wrote in his *Guardian* obituary. "If you did, you had nightmares."

A KEN RUSSELL FILM
STARRING ROGER DALTREY

LISZTOMANIA
Ⓜ

The erotic, exotic electrifying rock fantasy... *it out-Tommys "Tommy."*

ALSO STARRING SARA KESTELMAN · PAUL NICHOLAS AND FIONA LEWIS · GUEST STARS RINGO STARR · RICK WAKEMAN · MUSIC BY RICK WAKEMAN · EXECUTIVE PRODUCER SANDY LIEBERSON · PRODUCED BY ROY BAIRD AND DAVID PUTTNAM · WRITTEN AND DIRECTED BY KEN RUSSELL
A GOODTIMES ENTERPRISES PRODUCTION · TECHNICOLOR® From Warner Bros Ⓦ A Warner Communications Company

ORIGINAL SOUNDTRACK AVAILABLE ON A&M RECORDS

COPYRIGHT © WARNER BROS., INC.   LITHO.IN U.S.A.   3   75/249

opposite: Daltrey as the composer Franz Liszt in *Lisztomania*. Stills used to promote the film included one with The Who's singer astride a giant phallus.

above: A poster for *Lisztomania*, which stars Daltrey alongside Sara Kestelman, Paul Nicholas, and fellow musicians Ringo Starr and Rick Wakeman.

full of the kind of magnificent physical energy that usually wrecks a movie by calling attention to performance." He concluded by adding, "It's all fairly excessive and far from subtle, but in this case good taste would have been wildly inappropriate and a fearful drag."

Other reviewers followed the same line, and in *Rolling Stone* Jon Landau declared that Daltrey made a "sensational screen debut," an opinion that was pretty much unanimous.

"If nothing else, The Who would never be the same," wrote Ira Robbins, the editor/publisher of the alternative New York music paper *Trouser Press*, and a long-standing Who supporter. Commenting in hindsight, he added, "New doors opened to them, individually and collectively. The group gained a vast new audience too young or un-rock-conscious to have otherwise known of their work."

Elaborate premieres were held in Los Angeles and New York, where the newly refurbished subway station at 6th Avenue and 57th Street was chosen as the venue for reasons no one ever seemed to understand. Both parties were attended by a number of high-profile celebrities and socialites, none of whom were remotely connected to The Who; Townshend, for one, seemed conflicted by the contrast between what The Who used to stand for and what they seemed to be becoming in the light of Russell's movie.

The soundtrack album, a double LP, featured reworked versions of *Tommy* songs as they are heard in the film. Oliver Reed's singing voice makes even Keith Moon sound like a choirboy, as does that of Jack Nicholson, but Tina Turner's "Acid Queen" is stunning, as are the performances by Ann-Margret and Elton John, whose version of

"Pinball Wizard," backed by his own stage band, reached #7 in the UK singles chart in 1976. The album reached #21 in the UK charts, but in the long term it hasn't fared anywhere near as well as The Who's original LP.

The newly recorded songs all feature an abundance of synthesizer— as was becoming ever more prevalent in rock music—usually played by Townshend, and elaborate choral arrangements sung by backing vocalists brought in to offset the musical shortcomings of the tone-deaf actors. Several songs were radically reworked by the all-star band (which, ironically, included Kenney Jones, who would take over as The Who's drummer after Keith Moon's death in 1978). Entwistle reprised most of his bass work and also played all the horn parts. As well as guitar, keyboards, and synthesizer, Townshend produced the musical score—a thankless, time-consuming chore that drove him to the brink of a nervous breakdown.

From his reaction to the film, it might be assumed that Kit Lambert was also on the verge of a breakdown. Having harbored ambitions to produce a film of *Tommy* himself, not long after the film was released he sent out a press release announcing that he was preparing "final documents and far reaching legal action" against Robert Stigwood in connection with the film, for which he claimed to own the "world copyright." Nothing came of it, of course, other than Lambert's gradual estrangement from The Who, which Townshend, for one, regretted more than he cared to admit. Lambert died in 1981, ostensibly as a result of a brain hemorrhage following a fall down a staircase, but by then he was a broken man suffering from drug and alcohol abuse.

right: Townshend and his wife Karen attend the London premiere of *Tommy* at the Leicester Square Theatre, March 26, 1975.

opposite: Townshend, Daltrey, and Entwistle onstage at Live Aid, July 13, 1985. Under-rehearsed and far from match fit, The Who performed "My Generation," "Pinball Wizard," "Love Reign O'er Me," and "Won't Get Fooled Again." The live feed broke down during their set—the only time this occurred during the day.

right: Entwistle, Kenney Jones (who replaced Keith Moon in 1978), Daltrey, and Townshend backstage after their Live Aid performance, July 13, 1985.

The Kids Are Alright

When in 1973 The Who took *Quadrophenia* on the road, the new work occupied the lion's share of their set, with only "Pinball Wizard" and "See Me, Feel Me" from *Tommy* retained, both played following a medley of twelve *Quadrophenia* songs. For a variety of reasons—not least the need to perform it accompanied by prerecorded synthesizer parts—*Quadrophenia* never succeeded as well onstage as *Tommy*, and it would soon be dropped. Indeed, in this first phase, *Quadrophenia* was played only 32 times, compared with at least 160 concerts during 1969 and '70 that featured *Tommy* in (almost) its entirety.

On tour in 1975, the year that the *Tommy* film was released, The Who upped the *Tommy* quotient, featuring a medley of nine or ten of its songs in their sets. This number would fluctuate as, over the next twelve months, the group restructured their live sets to include other songs from an increasingly deep repertoire. At the Maple Leaf Gardens in Toronto, on October 21, 1976, the last concert Keith Moon would play before a paying audience, the set included nine *Tommy* songs. Among them, appropriately, was "Fiddle About," Moon's now legendary cameo as wicked Uncle Ernie.

When Kenney Jones took over on drums following Moon's death, The Who felt the need—for better or worse—to include new material from the two albums recorded with him, with the result that between 1979 and 1982, the importance of *Tommy* was considerably downgraded. By now, The Who had added a keyboard player to their stage band, and, at most of the shows with Jones, only "Pinball Wizard," "See Me, Feel Me," and, occasionally, "Sparks" were played.

At the end of 1982, The Who called it a day, though this wasn't made official until a year later, when Townshend issued a press statement to formally announce his departure from the group. They regrouped somewhat unsteadily for a one-off performance at Live Aid on July 13, 1985, in front of seventy-five thousand at Wembley Stadium and a worldwide TV audience of over one hundred million. The group's four-song set that day included "Pinball Wizard."

In 1989, twenty-five years after Moon's arrival cemented the "classic" lineup of the group, and twenty years since the release of *Tommy*, the three original members of The Who opted to observe the twofold anniversary with a massive tour of the United States, followed by a handful of dates in Britain. With Simon Phillips now on drums, they were augmented onstage by a further twelve musicians, mostly brass accompanists and backup singers. In deference to his damaged hearing, Townshend, looking smart in a dark suit, played an acoustic guitar throughout, with the lead guitar parts taken by Steve Bolton, who stood on the left of the stage next to Entwistle. The Kids Are Alright tour, as it was called, played to huge crowds in huge stadiums and grossed huge sums of money.

The shows ran to three hours or longer, with an interval; the first half was devoted to *Tommy*, usually featuring "Overture," "1921," "Amazing Journey," "Sparks," "Acid Queen," "Pinball Wizard," "Do You Think It's Alright?," "Fiddle About," "I'm Free," "Tommy's Holiday Camp," "We're Not Gonna Take It," and "See Me, Feel Me." The second half, which at most shows included a nostalgic segment wherein just Townshend, Daltrey, and Entwistle performed together without anyone else onstage, was a brisk run through a selection of The Who's best known songs.

For charity shows at the Radio City Music Hall in New York and the Universal Amphitheatre in Los Angeles, The Who performed *Tommy* in its entirety. In L.A. on August 24, 1989, an all-star lineup of guests played the various roles in the *Tommy* segment: Elton John as the Pinball Wizard, Phil Collins as Uncle Ernie, Patti LaBelle as the Acid Queen, Billy Idol as Cousin Kevin, and Steve Winwood as the Hawker.

The show easily sold out, with ticket sales totaling $2,050,782 from the crowd of 5,812, the proceeds benefitting three local charities and the Rock and Roll Hall of Fame. In addition, the performance was broadcast live as a pay-per-view television event and recorded for a subsequent triple-vinyl live album called *Join Together*, released in 1990. Cynical critics referred to this version of the group as the "Las Vegas Who," and older fans no doubt cringed at what they heard. The album hit the remainder bins within months of release. The US leg of the tour closed in Texas on September 3, and a month later this version of The Who played eight shows in Britain—four in Birmingham and four in London. The final date was at the Royal Albert Hall—now happy to accommodate The Who—on November 2. It was to be the last live concert that Townshend, Daltrey, and Entwistle played until 1996, when *Quadrophenia* was similarly revived.

Smashing the Mirror

A strand of entertainment that rock music was beginning to penetrate when *Tommy* first reared his head was musical theater, the most notable early example of which was *Hair*. A show about hippies, the counterculture, and the accompanying sexual revolution, it developed from a small off-Broadway show in New York, first staged in 1967,

to a full Broadway production that later reached London, where it ran for almost two thousand performances. Colorful, controversial, and irreverent, it opened the doors to other contemporary musicals in a sphere of showbiz that had lagged behind during the seemingly unstoppable advance of rock 'n' roll. *Hair* featured male and female nudity, and was in many ways responsible for the ending of censorship in the United Kingdom after Parliament overruled the Lord Chamberlain's decision not to issue the relevant license. Another important legacy of *Hair* was to expose redundant prudery in the United States, Britain, and elsewhere.

While *Hair* was essentially musical theater set to rock music instead of show tunes, the same cannot be said of the musicals scored by Andrew Lloyd Webber and Tim Rice, which, although "modern" in the sense that they first appeared in the seventies, harked back more to Stephen Sondheim and Rodgers and Hammerstein than forward to The Who and *Tommy*. Webber and Rice were at the forefront of what was termed "Godrock" with their own *Jesus Christ Superstar* and *Joseph and the Amazing Technicolor Dreamcoat*, both produced for the stage in 1970; and *Godspell*, with music and lyrics by Stephen Schwartz, first staged a year later. The only thing these shows had in common with *Tommy* was a spiritual message, albeit one more aligned to traditional religious beliefs than the teachings of an obscure Indian spiritual master whose simple message was "Don't worry, be happy," and who took a vow of silence at the age of thirty-one. Unlike *Tommy*, though, they were written specifically for the stage, so it comes as no real surprise that, in the fullness of time *Tommy*, too, would become a big-budget stage musical.

above: Townshend takes a final leap as he is joined onstage by members of the all-star cast at the close of the *Tommy* show at the Universal Amphitheatre, Los Angeles, August 22, 1989. *Left to right*: Billy Idol (Cousin Kevin), Patti LaBelle (Acid Queen), Elton John (Pinball Wizard), Phil Collins (Uncle Ernie), and Townshend.

the tommy variations
reissues and remasters

Over the years, The Who's original *Tommy* album has been reissued and upgraded numerous times, with improved sound, bonus tracks, and ever-expanding accompanying booklets. Here is a rundown of what are generally regarded as the most significant editions of *Tommy* to have been released.

The original double-vinyl package was released in the UK in May 1969 by Track Records (Track 613013/4). The album, which included an illustrated libretto, was issued with sides one and four on one disc and sides two and three on the other, thus enabling those who wanted to listen to it nonstop to flip the discs over only once on an auto-change record player. Two months earlier, "Pinball Wizard" b/w "Dogs Part II" (Track 604 027) had been released as a single.

In November 1970, a 33 ⅓ rpm *Tommy* EP was released (Track 2252 001) containing four songs, "Overture," "Christmas," "I'm Free," and "See Me, Feel Me," the latter an edit of the second half of "We're Not Gonna Take It" under the name that in the fullness of time became universally applied for the opera's climax. In 1972, the double LP was reissued on two separate discs, *Part 1* (sides one and two, Track 2406 007) and *Part 2* (sides three and four, Track 2406 008), with generic artwork but no libretto, presumably to make it more affordable. On this release, the label read *Tommy Revisited*.

Tommy by The London Symphony Orchestra and Chamber Choir with guest vocalists (ODE SP 88 001), produced by Lou Reizner, who had made his name working on Rod Stewart's first two solo albums, was released with much fanfare in November 1972. Initially a double vinyl album packaged in a box with a pinball motif on the cover, it was released as a single CD in 1989.

The *Tommy* film soundtrack (Polydor 9502), another double LP with a host of guests, came next, in March 1975. All tracks were produced by Pete Townshend and the movie's director, Ken Russell, apart from "Pinball Wizard," sung by Elton John, who insisted on using his own producer, Gus Dudgeon.

In 1981, the original *Tommy* appeared in *Phases* (Polydor 2675 216), a nine-album boxed set of The Who's catalogue up to *Who Are You*. It was first released on CD in 1984 as a two-disc set (Polydor 800 077-2), with a remixed single CD (Polydor 531 043-2) appearing in 1996 as part of a wholesale upgrading of The Who's back catalogue that occurred during the nineties. In 2004, it was reissued as a Deluxe Edition SACD hybrid (Polydor 9861011), a two-CD set with The Who's original recording of *Tommy* on disc one and seventeen outtakes and Townshend demos on disc two. This was followed in 2013 by a second double CD (Polydor 3747400), which alongside the remastered original recording of *Tommy* included *The Live Bootleg Album*, a recording of The Who performing *Tommy* onstage, almost all of which was recorded at the Capitol Theatre, Ottawa, on October 15, 1969.

This wasn't the first "official" live *Tommy* released by The Who, of course—just the first one with the *Tommy* artwork on the cover. A live rendering of Townshend's first full-length rock opera had first appeared, officially at least, on disc one of *Join Together*, a boxed album/CD package of The Who's 1989 reunion tour, and across the two CDs included in *The Who: Live at the Isle of Wight Festival 1970* (EDF CD 326), released by Castle Communications in 1996.

Reissued as a double CD in 2001, *Live at Leeds* includes *Tommy* on disc two, with the rest of the songs The Who played that memorable night—both before and after *Tommy*—on disc one, the producers having somewhat controversially elected to bisect the show rather than bisect *Tommy*. Moreover, when *Leeds* was released as a 40th Anniversary Super-Deluxe Collectors' Edition in 2010, the package

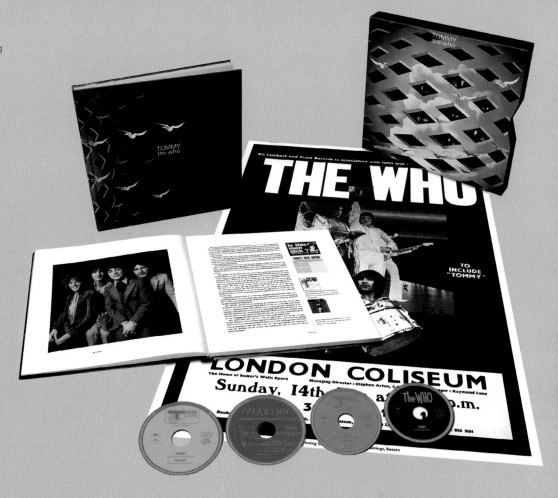

right: The 2013 Super DeLuxe *Tommy* boxed set. Costing around $100, this ultimate *Tommy* package includes four CDs, a book by Who insider Richard Barnes, and facsimiles of original artwork by Mike McInnerney.

included not just the original live *Tommy* recorded at Leeds University on February 14, 1970, but also the recording captured at Hull City Hall the following night.

In the meantime, there was the *Original Cast Recording* of the *Tommy* musical stage show (RCA Victor 09026 61874 2), a double CD produced by George Martin and released in 1993.

A vinyl reissue of *Tommy*—an exact two-LP replica—was included in the Studio Albums box set (Polydor 3715573) in 2012, and in 2013 as a standalone vinyl reissue (Polydor 3715749) plus a two-CD digipak (Polydor 3747400), which had the 2013 remastered original album on disc one and the *Live Bootleg* album on disc two, both taken from the 2013 Super Deluxe boxed set (Polydor 3747396).

This boxed set, the ultimate *Tommy* for fans and collectors, includes five CDs: the original 2013 remaster of the album, the Hi-Fidelity Pure Audio Blu-ray 5.1 mix, the Hi-Fidelity Pure Audio Blu-ray 2-channel stereo mix, a CD of twenty-five of Townshend's *Tommy* demos and outtakes, and the *Live Bootleg*. Also in the

package is a hardcover eighty-page book featuring unseen period photos, Pete's handwritten lyrics, and notes and memorabilia, an essay by Who archivist Richard Barnes, and a facsimile *Tommy* concert poster.

Perhaps the most unusual *Tommy* recording is *Tommy: A Bluegrass Opry* by The Hillbenders, released in 2015, which, as the title implies, is a bluegrass interpretation recorded with Townshend's blessing. A quintet from Springfield, Missouri, The Hillbenders not only pay homage to the music but also to Mike McInnerney's design with a crisscross lattice on the front cover, as befitting an all-acoustic recording.

The most recent *Tommy* recording is *Tommy Live at the Royal Albert Hall*, which was released by Eagle Rock/UMC in three-LP (EAGLP681) and two-CD (EDGCD680) editions in October 2017. Recorded on April 1, 2017, it was the first time ever that The Who—albeit now without either John Entwistle or Keith Moon—performed *Tommy* in its entirety, with no songs whatsoever left out.

As noted, there had been earlier theatrical productions in the past, and to these must be added another that played the Queen's Theatre in London's Hornchurch for six weeks in the spring of 1978. Directed by Paul Tomlinson, it transferred to the Queen's Theatre, Shaftesbury Avenue, opening in February 1979 for 118 performances. "With its confused messages of biblical and rock-drug references, and the absence of its original pop heroes, it received poor notices and managed just a three month run," reports the website *Over the Footlights: A History of British Theatre*.

In 1992 came a production on a far grander scale. The renamed *The Who's Tommy*, adapted for the stage by Townshend and La Jolla Playhouse director Des McAnuff, opened at La Jolla in San Diego, California, and was an instant commercial success, transferring to Broadway in the summer of 1993 and subsequently to London in 1997, and then Frankfurt. A box-office smash, it won three Tony Awards and has since gone on to have numerous revivals, principally in the United States and Britain, including one that toured the UK in 2017 with a cast that included disabled performers. The original London production won a Laurence Olivier Award for "Best Music Revival," with McAnuff picking up the "Best Director" award.

"*Tommy* is on Broadway," wrote Townshend approvingly, in an introduction to a book about the musical. "People love it and people hate it, but I am in a new kind of ecstasy. . . . And I have learned that there is a vital difference between the simple rock song and the conventional music theatre play—that it's necessary to bring a story to a conclusion, something you never have to do with rock 'n' roll."

Townshend wrote one new song for the production, "I Believe My

Own Eyes," a show tune–style duet between Tommy's mother and father that was slotted between "Tommy Can You Hear Me" and "Smash the Mirror." McAnuff created dialogue for all the characters, thus turning it into comic opera. The part of Tommy required three actors—one a child, one a boy, and the third an adult—while all and sundry were involved in lots of energetic dancing in front of backdrops in which pinball machines featured heavily. Show music–style vocals aside, much of the soundtrack sounded far more like an updated version of The Who's original album than the soundtrack to the movie. Where it varied was when an orchestra waded in, updating Lou Reizner's efforts with more sophisticated studio production.

The accompanying soundtrack album was produced by George Martin, whose name will forever be associated with The Beatles. "What I particularly love about this version of *Tommy* is that it has a Martin sound," wrote Townshend in sleeve notes accompanying the cast recording. "I'm not sure I realised that George Martin had a sound of his own, but he does. It is carried, I think, in the way he contributes all the traditional skills of studio recording developed in the fifties and early sixties and combined them with brand new techniques."

By now, *Tommy* had become as omnipresent as any musical you care to name, be it *Les Misérables*, *My Fair Lady*, or even *Mary Poppins*, and while it has some way to go in the all-time highest-grossing league, *Tommy* has made Pete Townshend enormously wealthy, above and beyond what he has earned as a member of The Who. Perhaps that goes some way to explaining why both Roger Daltrey and John Entwistle were reported to be less than charmed by *The Who's Tommy*.

above left: Entwistle and Daltrey at the opening of *The Who's Tommy* on Broadway, March 29, 1993.

above right: The cast of *The Who's Tommy* at Club USA, New York City, April 16, 1993.

above: Daltrey and Townshend lead the post-Entwistle Who during the half-time show at Super Bowl XLIV in Miami, February 7, 2010. Their twelve-minute set included truncated versions of "Pinball Wizard," "Baba O'Riley," "Who Are You," "See Me, Feel Me," and "Won't Get Fooled Again."

right: The bluegrass *Tommy* by The HillBenders, its cover based on Mike McInnerney's original sleeve design.

Still Seeing, Still Feeling

Omnipresent? On February 7, 2010, *Tommy*—or parts of it—were heard by the one hundred million American football fans who tuned in to the Super Bowl XLIV in Miami. The Who chose "Pinball Wizard" to open the halftime show, Townshend strumming those famous opening chords on an acoustic Gibson, and midway between "Who Are You" and "Won't Get Fooled Again," Daltrey, resplendent in a black-and-white striped blazer, intoned the equally famous "See Me, Feel Me" lines, for once stopping short of "Listening to You" due to the strict twelve-and-a-half-minute time limit.

Omnipresent? In 2011, Roger Daltrey took it on himself to perform *Tommy* with a band that included Simon Townshend, Pete's brother, at London's O2, and also at the Royal Albert Hall as a benefit for the Teenage Cancer Trust. Later the same year, he took the same show around Britain, Europe, and North America. "[It's] a *Tommy* show for today's audience from a different perspective," said Daltrey. Townshend added, "[It's] a faithful presentation of the original work as a backbone for a set of wider material. It is wonderful to hear the way Roger and his new band reinterpret the old songs."

Omnipresent? When you key "Tommy by The Who" into Google, you are informed there are 262,000,000 results, though, in reality, once you get past page twelve, the clothes guru Tommy Hilfiger starts to trespass into the entries. Still, there are separate fields for *Tommy* the movie, *Tommy* the musical, *Tommy* songs, *Tommy* can you hear me, *Tommy* pinball wizard, and, of course, Uncle Ernie, who can also be found in Wiki Villains, a site marked "Mature: recommended for those ages eighteen and over." His occupation is given as "church assistant," which in the light of recent scandals of an ecclesiastical nature seems rather fitting, and his hobby "manipulating and intimidating children." There's even a picture of Keith Moon looking very grubby indeed.

Omnipresent? In May of 2016, I came across a poster for a bluegrass version of *Tommy* to be performed live by an American quintet from Springfield, Missouri, called The HillBenders at the Union Chapel in Islington in North London. Their CD of *Tommy* had been on release for just under a year, its yellow cover an almost exact facsimile of Mike McInnerney's original blue cover for The Who, except that the crisscross lattice on the front is made from what looks like beechwood, as befitting an acoustic recording. The arrangements hardly vary from The Who's original. In many respects, the stand-up bass makes up for the lack of percussion, though someone taps the body of an acoustic here and there. Guitarist Jim Rea follows Pete's lines closely—on acoustic, of course—and the rapidly picked banjo throughout seems perfectly natural, once you've got your head around the fact that this is a bluegrass interpretation. The guitar/banjo opening on "Pinball Wizard" is particularly effective. Toward the end, as one of the quintet offers up Roger's "See Me, Feel Me" plea, it verges on the operatic, and when all five chime in on the closing lines—"Listening to You"— the banjo speeds up like an express train.

Dedicating their record to "the power of The Who," The HillBenders are clearly in awe of them, and their *Tommy* is without doubt another respectful tribute, in homage to them, if you like. I spotted a picture online of Townshend with the five guys, so we can assume the creator of *Tommy* has given them the green light. They did him proud.

> " I personified Tommy. I was the guy who used to play the part. I played the damn part for five years. I slogged my balls off around the world, sweating it out. People thought I *was* Tommy. I used to get called Tommy in the street."
>
> Roger Daltrey to *Goldmine*, July 8, 1994

Perhaps this hillbilly version went some way to explaining why, in 2016, Roger Daltrey began talking about how The Who were planning to perform an all-acoustic *Tommy* during the series of shows that he promotes annually at the Royal Albert Hall for the Teenage Cancer Trust. In the event, this didn't happen, Townshend commenting, "Roger often sidles up to me and says, 'I think *Tommy* would be so great done acoustic.' I reply, 'So what you're saying, Rog, is that you want me to sit for an hour and a half and accompany you on my acoustic guitar? For an hour and a half, while you noodle on around on vocals?' There's a quick 'Fuck off!' to that idea. An unplugged show? I'll save it for the charity gigs or the occasional solo shows."

The Who, as they were configured in 2017, did perform two *Tommy* shows at the RAH on March 30 and April 1, playing the entire twenty-four-song cycle, including even "Underture." A similar program was performed in arenas at Liverpool, Manchester, Glasgow, Sheffield, and Birmingham in the week that followed.

Finally, in June and July of 2018, Daltrey took The Who's touring band, absent of Townshend, on the road in North America to play *Tommy* in its entirety in eleven cities where he was additionally accompanied by local symphony orchestras. "It's going to be magnificent with the orchestra," Daltrey told *Rolling Stone* magazine before the tour started. "It won't be sloppy strings, I assure you. The band is so solid underneath. And we stay faithful to the record. We treat it with the respect that you'd treat a Mozart opera."

The man who more than anyone identified as Tommy had been made a CBE in the New Year's Honours List at the end of 2004, but when he knelt before the queen the following February, he no longer looked anything like the man who first became Tommy on The Who's stages in 1969 and 1970. The golden curls were shorn long ago, the tasseled suede coat long since mothballed, and when he posed with his medal and six-year-old granddaughter, he wore gold-rimmed glasses and a blue pinstriped suit over a white shirt and azure blue tie. Still, as the decade that followed would prove, Roger Daltrey's commitment to the music composed by his musical partner of over fifty years standing, the rock opera that turned him into a rock God, remained undimmed.

At the Races

Tommy was released in May of 1969, and was spinning around on my record deck a month later. That same double-vinyl LP is still in my collection, a bit shabby now, its cover torn, the libretto lacking staples, and, as for the actual discs—well, I doubt even a charity shop would accept them.

Over the years, that original copy has been joined by a pristine vinyl edition and several CDs, but when I began to write this I got it out again and played it, scratches and all. It took me back to the summer of 1969, which was also when I saw The Who for the first time, on Saturday, August 9, at the National Jazz and Blues Festival, held on Plumpton Racecourse near Lewes in Sussex.

A friend who worked on one of the bars got me onto the site on the premise that I'd help with washing glasses. I probably did, too, but not on the Saturday night when The Who were playing. By today's standards, the festival at Plumpton was small-time—perhaps twenty-five thousand attending at the most—which made it fairly easy to push my way down

right: Daltrey, flanked by his sister Gillian and wife Heather, with granddaughter Lily, shows off his CBE outside Buckingham Palace, February 9, 2005.

toward the front, to the right of the stage where Pete Townshend stood. That summer, *Tommy* hadn't been off my turntable in weeks, so I knew the songs well, and now here they were, a matter of yards from me, performing their rock opera virtually in its entirety. At the climax, as they sang about listening to us and getting the music, I thought The Who performing *Tommy* was the most wonderful thing I'd seen in my whole life. Two weeks, later The Who would do the same thing in front of a crowd almost twenty times bigger at Woodstock, sealing their reputation as one of the world's greatest ever live rock bands. Back at Plumpton, amid the cheers that followed their set, I decided there and then that I wanted to be a part of this.

The Monday after the Plumpton show, back in the newspaper office in Slough where I worked, I was restless. I didn't like wearing a suit and tie, and I didn't like getting my hair cut—both of which were prerequisites for newspaper reporters who were supposed to look smart. Each week I bought *Melody Maker* and read it cover to cover, which is how, in October, I spotted an advert in its back pages for a job on the editorial staff. I somehow got an afternoon off and went into London, to *MM*'s offices on Fleet Street, for an interview with the paper's editor, Ray Coleman. When he asked me to name my favorite group I said, "The Who."

Ray smiled. "Good choice," he replied.

A week or two later, Ray's secretary called to tell me I hadn't got the job. Back in Slough, I toiled away at the *Evening Mail* with decreasing enthusiasm, not quite sure where I was going next. Then, in the New Year, I got another call from Ray Coleman. There was another vacancy. Was I still interested? Was I ever . . .

> We'll have a couple of weeks off, John will take his dogs out for a walk, then we'll all sort of get together in a boozer, all sort of get drunk and decide absolutely nothing . . . but eventually it'll all get thrown together—that's how we wrote most of *Tommy*, in a pub opposite the recording studio."
>
> Keith Moon to *Crawdaddy!*, December 5, 1971

On April 27, 1970, I went to see The Who again, taking a girl I wanted to impress to the Civic Hall in Dunstable, Bedfordshire, where they played *Tommy* again and Pete smashed a guitar. That night was the last time in ten years I would have to buy myself a ticket for a rock concert. A week later, two weeks before my twenty-third birthday, I joined the staff of *Melody Maker*.

Oddly enough, the next time I saw The Who was also in Dunstable, on July 27, this time as a *Melody Maker* reviewer. "They almost lifted the roof off this architectural marvel as they pounded away for nearly two hours," I wrote in the paper's "Caught in the Act" column. "Billed now as 'the most exciting stage act in the world' they lived up to their name. The Who are unique in the excitement they manage to create—and this is almost entirely due to Pete Townshend's leaping and jumping as he treats guitar and amps with little or no respect."

The following Friday, two days after my review appeared in *MM*, the phone on my desk rang.

"Hello."

"Is that Chris?"

"Yes."

"Keith here. Keith Moon. From The Who."

Indeed, I thought. *Is there any other?*

"I'm just ringing to say thanks for the nice review of the group you wrote."

"Err . . . it's a pleasure, Keith. I love The Who."

"So do I. We must have a drink sometime, dear boy."

"I'd love to."

"Meet me in La Chasse, or the Speakeasy.[11] Come and say hello."

"I will, I promise. Bye."

I was flabbergasted. I hadn't been at *MM* for three months, and I'd written positively about a few other acts, yet none had called to thank me. Now here was Keith Moon, a member of a band that was far and away the most skilled, successful, and popular of all the groups I'd reviewed, calling up to thank me for a good review. Neither he nor The Who actually *needed* a good review to help their career at this stage—unlike some of the others—yet Keith saw fit to call.

The next time we met, Keith invited me to be his guest at a Who concert at the Hammersmith Palais, in October. On the night we were driven there in his lilac Rolls-Royce, which pulled up outside the front doors in full view of fans waiting in line to get in. When Keith stepped out of the car, the crowd parted like the red sea to allow him to walk through, cheering him as he went by. I was by his side. I imagined it was like walking through the gates of Graceland alongside Elvis. That night, I met the other three members of The Who for the first time.

They played *Tommy* again that night, as they did on the fourth occasion I saw the group that year, at London's Roundhouse on December 20, with Elton John. I saw The Who with Keith on drums another thirty times over the next six years, often in situations where I was backstage and socializing with them before and after the shows, the final occasion on August 7, 1976, in Jacksonville, on the coast of northern Florida. They remain the greatest live band I've ever seen, and some of the greatest shows I ever saw were those when they played *Tommy* in 1969 and '70.

> "It's not exactly the clearest plot is it? Some of the songs just don't fit it in any plot. But I'll tell you what, when you play *Tommy* in its entirety, it's so complete, it's so wonderful. The simplicity of it. The power in the lyrics. The journey. It builds and builds . . . it was genius. And Pete deserves everything he got from it."
>
> Roger Daltrey, *Thanks a Lot Mr. Kibblewhite: My Story*, 2018

Bathed in Glory

On June 26, 2015, The Who performed before an audience of sixty-five thousand or more in London's Hyde Park. It wasn't really The Who, just Roger and Pete, with Zak Starkey, Ringo's son, on drums; Pino Palladino, ace session player, on bass; Simon Townshend, Pete's brother, on extra guitar; and three keyboard players. Keith and John would no doubt be gratified to know that it took six extra musicians to replace them.

Playing to sixty-five thousand people in central London's largest park, where there is a strict curfew and noise levels are monitored so as not to offend the multimillionaires living nearby, The Who were strangely subdued, not that the audience seemed to care. But I wasn't alone in noticing that the show didn't really catch fire until the sun set, which, happily, coincided with the *Tommy* segment.

"Amazing Journey" seemed to galvanize things, and "Sparks" / "Underture"—its churning opening rumble suspended, brilliantly, while Roger riffed on the "Captain Walker didn't come home" lines—was spectacular, as it always was and still is. The audience around me seemed to feel it, too, all of us lifted to a higher level as those well-known crescendos and octave drops filled the night. Pete was feeling it, too, improvising on the chords, feeling his way along the fretboard of his guitar to harmonics that fed Zak, who held back unexpectedly and then tumbled back into the rhythmic cascades, challenging Pete, eye to eye, just like when Keith was up there with him. Momentarily, this was The Who as they used to be, that spontaneous touch of greatness, back to the time when they really were the best in the business.

Twilight arrived as Pete played the descending chords of "Pinball's" intro, triggering another crowd eruption. Although an old stager like me missed John's dramatic bass tones, all sixty-five thousand of us were behind Roger as the young boy who played the silver ball, and the night, finally, was as alive as it was ever going to get. It was dark when Roger intoned the famous "See Me, Feel Me" lines and Pete led this eight-man Who band into the *Tommy* hymn to turn a good show into another great one.

Two nights later, much the same thing happened at Glastonbury in front of a much bigger—and much younger—audience. They pitched in with the sort of aggression you don't really expect from performers of their age, Pete windmilling furiously, Roger in good voice, and the rest of them, especially Zak, determined to follow Pete's example.

Toward the end of their set, the lights dimmed, and Townshend began the frenzied flamenco strum that heralds "Pinball Wizard." A huge roar once more greeted that descending chord sequence. Everyone, young and old, seemed to recognize it. It was as if "Pinball Wizard" was on that week's Radio 1 playlist. Boys not yet born when Keith Moon was alive punched the air with their fists. Beautiful young girls in their teens or early twenties, either at the front or perched on their boyfriends' shoulders, sang along, deliriously happy. It morphed into "See Me, Feel Me," and, just as at Woodstock forty-six years earlier, there was a hush as Daltrey intoned those famous lines. Then Townshend hammered on the suspended chord that leads into the chorus: "Listening to you, I get the music."

Up came the lights, and, yet again, *Tommy* was bathed in glory, and his disciples, the millions at his feet, got the story.

right and overleaf: Daltrey and Townshend lead The Who—now comprising eight musicians—onstage at Glastonbury, June 28, 2015. This was the group's second Glastonbury appearance, following on from their rain-drenched set in 2007.

endnotes

1 In contrast, Led Zeppelin played just 516 shows in their entire twelve-year career between 1968 and 1980.

2 The Beatles had the luxury of being able to spend hour after hour in the studio—in their case EMI's Abbey Road—working on songs until they were satisfied. This was due wholly to EMI's realization that The Beatles was a goose that laid golden eggs, and it was therefore in its financial interest to grant the group unlimited free studio time in a studio the label owned anyway.

3 In the film of *Tommy* this is switched, i.e. his mother's lover murders Tommy's father. The stage show version reverts to the original story.

4 Strangely, this album's production team chose to insert three songs ("I'm Free," "Tommy's Holiday Camp," and "We're Not Gonna Take It") from a show at Swansea on June 12, 1976, in place of the versions played at Ottawa. This might have been because the Ottawa tapes had deteriorated, but there was a noticeable difference in texture between these songs and the rest of the CD. It was probably hoped that no one would notice, but many fans, including this writer, felt it was an insult to their intelligence.

5 In the seventies, vinyl reissues of the album began using a version of this track with an alternate vocal. The early CD releases continued to do so as well. The MFSL "Gold" and remastered CDs have reverted to the original.

6 The only interruption came when Yippie spokesman Abbie Hoffman walked onstage to protest against the jailing of White Panther John Sinclair. "Fuck off my fucking stage," yelled Townshend, before hitting Hoffman with his guitar so hard he fell off the stage into the pit below.

7 At the time, this did not appear to be entirely positive. The DipAD was the first step toward academic awards that would require affiliation to larger academic institutions and their bureaucratic structures. Concern was expressed for the survival of the unique qualities of the mono-technic art-college system. The art college had always attracted students from a wide range of backgrounds and experience. Academic filtering could change this, and it did. The National Advisory Council on Art Education optimistically declared that all art schools would be free to work out their own ideas. In practice, the pre-Diploma established common practice across the country. There was concern about art students donning cap and gown to receive degrees as the DipAD transformed later into BA degree awards.

8 The documentary DVDs include *The Kids Are Alright* (1979), *Who's Better Who's Best* (1988), *30 Years of Maximum R&B Live* (2003), and *Amazing Journey: The Story of The Who* (2007).

9 This rivalry was eventually settled in Curbishley's favor.

10 Elton John auctioned off the boots in 1988. They were purchased by R. Griggs Group Ltd, and are permanently displayed at the Shoe Collection at the Northampton Museum and Art Gallery.

11 La Chasse and the Speakeasy were both private members clubs frequented by musicians and people from the music industry.

selected bibliography

Atkins, John. *The Who On Record* (McPharland & Co., 2000)

Baba, Meher. *Discourses* (Sheriar Press, 1967)

Barnes, Richard, and Townshend, Pete. *The Story of Tommy* (Eel Pie Publishing, 1997)

Barnes, Richard. Liner notes to *Tommy* (Polydor Records, 1996 reissue)

Barnes, Richard. *The Who: Maximum R&B* (Plexus, 1982)

Blake, Mark. *Pretend You're in a War: The Who and the Sixties* (Aurum Press, 2014)

Buckley, David. *Elton John: The Biography* (Andre Deutsch, 2006)

Charlesworth, Chris, and Hanel, Ed. *The Complete Guide to the Music of The Who* (Omnibus Press (1994; 2004)

Charlesworth, Chris. *Townshend: A Career Biography* (Proteus, 1984)

Clark, Steve. *The Who in Their Own Words* (Omnibus Press, 1979)

Cohn, Nik. *Awopbopaloobop Alopbamboom)* (Paladin, 1969)

Crippa, Elena, and Williamson, Beth. *Basic Design* (Tate. 2013)

De Leon, Delia. *The Ocean of Love: My Life with Meher Baba* (Sheriar Press, 1991)

Fletcher, Tony. *Dear Boy: The Life of Keith Moon* (Omnibus Press, 1998)

Green, Jonathon. *Days in the Life* (Pimlico, 1998)

Gregory, Richard L. *Eye and Brain: The Psychology of Seeing* (Princeton University Press, 1998)

Hanel, Ed. *The Who: The Illustrated Discography* (Omnibus Press, 1981)

Hayes, Colin. *Grammar of Drawing for Artists and Designers* (Studio Vista, 1969)

Home, Stewart. *The Assault on Culture: Utopian Currents from Lettrisme to Class War* (AK Press, 1991)

Horn, Gerd-Rainer. *The Spirit of '68: Rebellion in Western Europe and North America, 1956–1976* (Oxford University Press, 2007)

Larkin, Colin (ed.). *The Encyclopedia of Popular Music* (Oxford University Press, 2006)

Marsh, Dave. *Before I Get Old: The Story of The Who* (Plexus, 1983)

McMichael, Joe, and Lyons, Jack. *The Who Concert File* (Omnibus Press, 1997)

Mellor, David Alan, and Gervereau, Laurent. *The Sixties: Britain and France, 1962–1973, The Utopian Years* (Philip Wilson Publishers Limited, 1997)

Miles, Barry. *London Calling: A Countercultural History of London Since 1945* (Atlantic Books, 2010)

Motion, Andrew. *The Lamberts: George, Constance, and Kit* (Chatto & Windus, 1986)

Neill, Andy, and Kent, Matt. *Anyway, Anyhow Anywhere: The Complete Chronicle of The Who 1958–1978* (Barnes & Noble, 2002)

Parola, Rene. *Optical Art: Theory and Practice* (Dover Publications, Inc., 1996)

Rogan, Johnny. *The Kinks: The Sound and the Fury* (Elm Tree Books, 1984)

Smith, Larry David. *Pete Townshend: The Minstrel's Dilemma* (Praeger, 1999)

Townshend, Pete. Liner notes to *Scoop* (1983), *Another Scoop* (1987), and *Scoop 3* (2001)

Townshend, Pete. *The Decade of The Who* (Wise Publications, 1984)

Townshend, Pete. *Who I Am* (Harper Collins, 2012)

Various. *The Who's Tommy: The Musical* (Pantheon Books, 1993)

Warwick, Neil, Kutner, Jon, and Brown, Tony. *The Complete Book of the British Charts* (Omnibus Press, 2004)

The websites rocksbackpages.com and thewho.com were also consulted.

index

picture credits

Every effort has been made to trace the copyright holders of the artworks in this book. In order for any errors or omissions to be corrected in future editions, please contact Elephant Book Company.

Front cover and all chapter openers © Mike McInnerney.

7: Getty Images/Tim P Whitby; 9, 89T, 97, 139BR, 144, 146T: Alamy/Pictorial Press; 11, 21B, 51L, 51R, 52, 99, 159: Trinifold; 12: Rex/Shutterstock/Dezo Hoffman; 15T, 147: Alamy/Keystone Pictures USA; 15B: Getty Images/M Stroud/Express/ Hulton Archive; 16: Getty Images/Ted Streshinksy Archive; 17, 24R: Getty Images/ Adam Ritchie; 18: Getty Images/Stanley Bielecki/ASP; 21T, 23, 31L, 31R, 42L, 45R, 90, 101BL, 135L, 139TR, 141TL, 141TR: Private Collection; 22L: Alamy/Tracks Images; 22R: Richard Barnes; 24L, 26L, 39L, 40R, 86, 87, 104R, 107T, 107B, 111T, 111B, 112T, 112B 114, 115, 116L, 116R, 119L, 119TR, 119BR, 120L 120R, 163: Mike McInnerney; 25, 57, 69R, 108R: Alamy/Pictorial Press/Tony Gale; 26R, 83: International Times; 27L: Dudley Edwards; 27R, 39R, 104L: Mike McInnerney, Dudley Edwards/OMtentacle; 29L, 29R, 38: Beloved Archives; 32, 40L, 48, 53, 58, 59, 65, 103, 109TR: Getty Images/Chris Morphet; 33: Rex/Shutterstock/ Bruce Fleming; 35, 134: Getty Images/Bettman; 37: Alamy/PictureLux/The Hollywood Archive; 41: McInnerney Archive; 45L, 63R, 150: Alamy/Everett Collection; 47: Rex/Shutterstock/Mike Randolph; 54, 61, 62, 70, 72, 74, 75, 81, 82: Iconic Images/Baron Wolman; 55L: Getty Images/Michael Ochs Archives; 60: Getty Images/Chris Walter/Wireimage; 63L: Alamy/Kenneth Walton; 66: Alamy/Lebrecht Music and Arts; 67: Getty Images/Jan Olofsson; 69L: Alamy/ D. Hurst; 77, 146B: Alamy/Moviestore Collection; 78: Alamy/United Archives GmbH; 79: Getty Images/Ralph Ackerman; 85, 95: Alamy/Trinity Mirror/Mirrorpix; 89B: Rex Shutterstock/Associated Newspapers; 91: Rex/Shutterstock/David Graves; 93: Getty Images/Visualeyes Archive; 94: Karen Townshend; 95: Getty Images/Keystone; 98: Getty Images/Jack Mitchell; 101TL: Alamy/Granger Historical Picture Archive; 101R: istockphoto/George Peters; 102, 137R, 143TL, 143B: Getty Images/Michael Putland; 106: Alamy/Neil Setchfield—Vintage; 108L: Rex/Shutterstock/David Magnus; 109TL: Getty Images/RB; 109BL, 154: Getty Images/Photoshot; 109BR: Getty Images/Jack Robinson; 121: Radio Times/ Don Smith; 122: Getty Images/Michael Ochs Archives/Jim Steinfeldt; 125: Getty Images/Ron Howard; 126: Getty Images/Photoshot/Monitor Picture Library; 128: Rex Shutterstock/Brian Moody; 129L, 152: Rex Shutterstock; 129R, 137BL, 166T: Chris Charlesworth Archive; 131: Rex/Shutterstock/Robert Stigwood Prods/ Hemdale/Kobal; 132: Alamy/Moviestore Collection; 133, 143TR: Getty Images/ Gijsbert Hanekroot; 135R: Alamy/Granger Historical Picture Archive/Richard Busch; 136: Alamy/MARKA; 137TL, 139L: Alamy/sjvinyl; 141B: Getty Images/ Peter Still; 145: Alamy/courtesy Granamour Weems Collection; 149: Alamy/ TCD/Prod.DB; 151: Getty Images/Redferns; 153: Rex Shutterstock/Andre Csillag; 155, 157: Getty Images/Dave Hogan; 156: Rex Shutterstock/Richard Young; 161L: Getty Images/Ron Galella, Ltd.; 161R: Getty Images/Steve Eichner; 162: Getty Images/Kevin Mazur; 165: Rex/Shutterstock/Tim Rooke; 166B: Getty Images/K&K Ulf Kruger OHG; 169T: Alamy/classic/Roger Cracknell 01; 169B: Getty Images/Samir Hussein; 170/171: Getty Images/Oli Scarff.

acknowledgments

Chris Charlesworth: I am grateful to Ed Hanel, Matt Kent, and Andy Neill for their depth of Who knowledge, and to Lisa Seckler-Roode and Tony Fletcher for telling me things I didn't want to know. Thanks also to Richard Evans for bringing me up to date on recent Who releases, and Mike Tremaglio for supplying images. Finally, thanks to my oldest friend Chris Whincup for getting me into the Plumpton Festival, without whom I might have gone to the pub that night in 1969.

Mike McInnerney: I would like to thank Pete Townshend for his time and patient efforts with my varied requests and Karen Townshend for her thoughtful and entertaining conversations. My appreciation to Dinah Lone for her support and clarity in all matters digital as well as inspiration. My thanks also to Richard "Barney" Barnes for providing personal memories.

editorial credits

Editorial Director: Will Steeds
Project Editor: Tom Seabrook
Picture Researcher: Sally Claxton